SILENT CRIES

from the Hearts of Alcoholics and Addicts

W. Lionel Carrega

Copyright © 2015 Wentworth Lionel Carrega

Publisher: Carrega & Carreras
Brooklyn, New York
wentworthcarrega@yahoo.com

ISBN: 978-0-692-02684-7 (sc)
ISBN: 978-1-4834-3525-1 (e)

First Edition

To Dad who insisted on inquiry for an understanding.

Having worked many years inside NYC government, wading neck-deep through red tape and regulations, I was fortunate enough to have touched upon a population largely viewed by the same light. I saw something different; I saw another side.

What follows are the problems witnessed; testimonies heard, ideas expressed, and TRUTHS!

Everyone has an opinion, and is entitled to express it. Yet, an opinion's value is solely based in those who will hear it and give credence. Inquiry unearths information, regardless of nature, further fueling the need for knowledge.

Contents

PREFACE...xi
ACKNOWLEDGEMENTS...xv
ABOUT THIS WORK...xvii
INTRODUCTION xxi

ABANDONMENT 1
THE PROCESS...18
THE CRIES..22
THE PROBLEM 75
THE THOUGHT..79
OBSERVATIONS..82
THE LEXICON 90
THE LEXICON AT WORK...92
THE GAME 95
The DSM 5 97
GLORIA'S.. 104
HERE DO WE GO FROM HERE?.. 120
FIGHTING THE DEMONS 124
ASSUMPTIONS OF RECOVERY 131
THE ANSWER... 135
MYTHS... 138
THE CORTICORTROPIN RELEASE FACTOR (CRF) 152
HEROIN & PRESCRIBED NARCOTICS PILLS 155
SUBSTANCE ABUSE BY OLDER ADULTS 167
MARIJUANA IN TODAY'S CHANGING WORLD............................ 170
E-CIGARETTES- INSIDUOUS TECHNOLOGY 180

REASONS TO LEGALIZE 186
MEDICINAL MARIJUANA 194
ALERT 200
SUMMATION 203

BIBLIOGRAPHY 209
ABOUT THE AUTHOR 213

PREFACE

It is the author's hope this work be used by associates, friends, and relatives who are witnessing alcoholic and drug dependent behaviors on an ongoing basis and trying to make sense of these behaviors. It can also be used by the inquisitive mind that listens directly to the voices coming from the characters herein engulfed with substance abuse and dependency.

Sections can be read independently of the whole. Those sections read can be linked to continue the discussion with the same themes—alcoholism and drug addiction. For emphasis, the themes take on a seemingly repetitious manner for reinforcement and context, so that readers can use the information to draw inferences and relate to the subject.

The hope is, by stripping away the façade of the alcoholic and drug addict, the reader may come away with a sense of their world. This accounting clears the smoke for the reader to get an understanding of the everyday struggles and efforts expended by alcoholics and drug abusers in their attempts to be freed from the jaws of their addiction and dependency.

This book is not a diagnostic tool. Rather, it attempts to minimize scientific jargon so that it can be easily read by everyone. It gives a glimpse into the newly confusing task, created by the [1] DSM5 (Diagnostic Statistical Manual of Mental Disorder 5th Ed.) in 2014 for clinicians and those working in the helping professions. It also blends contradictory scientific data from experts and researchers in the field of substance abuse while bringing to the forefront the physiological link to addiction.

Because of contradictory and inconclusive information on the linkage of unadulterated marijuana to addiction, if any can be documented, a different picture is herein presented. The medicinal and the economic realities of marijuana, from a changing world of evolving ideas, are presented.

What follows are the intimate revelations made by alcoholics and drug addicts, while alive and were in recovery, as defined by them from decades of cognitive use and abuse of, licit and illicit substances. The individuals were from every socio economic, educational, professional, and racial backgrounds. Most of the individuals who opened the doors into their lives and worlds met the author during his tenure in departments of [2] New York City Social Services, and in particular, at the [3] Administration for Children's Services.

It was a journey.

The great majority of alcoholics and drugs addicts understood addiction and dependency from what they were taught by experts whose focus delved specifically into their psychological issues. Most became engaged in phases of rehabilitation, with intermittent success, while issues in their lives continued to vary in magnitude.

The book presents living proof of the little progress that was made by many during their involvement in programs of rehabilitation. For those who were clinically engaged, they described counseling as, "good information gathering" that did little to stymie the twin problems that they continued to face on a daily basis. The lack of true progress made by this population, who were engaged in therapeutic phases, remained addicted and by extension, it implied that a void existed and exists in the current assumptions of addiction and dependency. Because of the apparent void, this book presents another option, thrown into the mix, to further the discussion of alcoholism and drug addiction.

The author extrapolated a few poignant examples, from those who were interviewed in the past having since departed to the other world. Many of the revelations herein allegedly were never divulged by the departed to their assigned counselor/s, psychiatrist, psychologist, or to any persons of authority. Had their revelations been made known, there would have been punitive actions with lasting negative effects by advocates and bureaucracies. These individuals, while they were alive, presented documentation from programs verifying that they were in recovery and had been participating in numerous programs for an average of ten years. Some of them viewed these programs as effective.

Those who chose to end their involvement with programs accepted a title of functional alcoholic or functional drug user. For this population, acceptance of being trapped without lasting change brought reality to their situation. Most who accepted such title met their needs, and those of their families, while continuing their indulgences. Many resigned to thinking there is something else beyond the programs.

Some concluded that a good and meaningful support system was the key to their survival. Because of that recognition and the importance of a good support system, they remained in programs despite their dislike of continuing as participants. This population accepted the title functional and maintained stability with assistance from a network of supportive individuals.

For the reader who recognizes dependency behaviors presented in this book, hopefully assistance would be sought. Should the reader consider theirself a functional alcoholic or drug addict who has never explored alternative approaches, the hope is you may acquire new insight. The decision of what type of action to take remains with the abuser.

ACKNOWLEDGEMENTS

Uncovering the public façade of the alcoholic or drug addict became a bit of an obsession that needed an outlet to expose the real person. Without being a keen observer, these stories could not have been told; hopefully in a vivid manner which lays out their reality as it is presented.

The motivation behind this book came directly from colleagues with whom I shared a working relationship for two decades at ACS (Administration for Children's Services, NYC). Those colleagues planted the seeds for inquiry through lending their keen years of experience and formal training. Although, at times, disagreement and opinions were sharp and engulfed with probing questions, it was a true learning experience.

The client population at the Administration for Children Services provided the driving force to complete this project with a focus on alcoholics. Despite the focus of this work being alcoholism, the role that drug addiction played in their lives will be discussed.

The new phenomenon of substance abuse by the elderly, and heroin emerging from a hiatus will be presented. Moreover, a new look at the reality of marijuana, not as a gateway drug, as being currently stressed, but as a reality which can be incorporated into daily life with parameters and responsibility.

There are many anonymous persons to whom this work is dedicated, and with the hope that those who are afflicted with alcoholism and dependency can see their efforts at rehabilitation through another set of lenses. I hope that seeing, through reflections, brings about positive actions in the quest for sobriety.

It is the hope that the reporting of these incidents brings to light the difficulties of abusers as they saw themselves in the pages that follow. These reported incidents lends itself to further inquiry into the human propensity to use and abuse substances.

Thanks to those who patiently read the chapters and raised questions for further discussions on addiction and alcoholism. Their input was invaluable. To the friends and colleagues whom I wanted most to read at least some parts of the manuscript and present counterbalancing arguments and questions, their absence of input was attributed to occupational and personal family responsibilities- I understand. Yet, their verbal comments and input on the issues herein were meaningful.

Without the help of my good friend Butch and his technical skills, this project would not have been possible. He was invaluable in researching images for the cover, and doing the tedious task of corroborating bibliographical pieces.

Thanks to the many whose time was invaluable during editing and reviewing prior to publication.

This work offers an interpretation of alcoholism that deemphasizes the psychological approach and emphasizes a physiological slant. Myths of alcoholism and drug addiction are presented to add clarity to the issues for further discussion. It does not deny the importance of psychological factors contributing to alcoholism. Rather, it provides an insight and explanation of other contributing behaviors that are not made an issue of importance in today's rehabilitation programs.

This work is not about negative or positive, licit or illicit drugs, or its effects, although it encompasses all. Rather, it intrudes in a raw manner to lift the façade of the affliction.

ABOUT THIS WORK

This work is the product of many years of encounters with clients, associates, friends, prior to and during my tenure in a government helping agency. During those years of face to face contacts with the aforementioned population, in their environment, and in unfamiliar territory, challenges were presented and many questions were raised.

Those personal encounters dissipated and stopped with the passage of time and subsequent death. Despite the latter, I ventured into the unknown world of alcoholics and addicts, away from the facades presented in clinical situations or environments dictated by authority. In those situations, there were no pretentions and true personalities were revealed.

Most of these clients were found to be calculating and clever in their own way, and possessing qualities that could only be discovered by an observer who was free of the human instinct to judge. Just being an observer to behaviors of the addict and alcoholic gave meaning to human susceptibility and not a conclusion. Others, despite being smart, displayed behaviors congruous with alcoholism and drug addiction.

However, observing significant persons indulging in alcohol and drugs abuse, and with whom communication and interaction took place regularly, caused the mind to be jolted with questions. I remained an observer.

It was quite disconcerting to remain neutral as limitless quantities of alcohol and drugs were bought with meager earnings, just to satisfy their dependencies. However, consuming alcohol or drugs in a jovial manner, while neglecting responsibilities of the family, became the challenge of addressing their behaviors tactfully.

The thought of confronting their behaviors without being abrasive or judgmental or dictatorial or directional carried an uneasiness that threatened to truncate long established relationships that were built over several decades. It was the challenge of another dimension and too close for comfort.

Those years of observing have been a learning experience in human behaviors. Largely, the learning came from interpreting silent behaviors; body language that spoke volumes with meaning. My silence, and the abusers' body language, was some of the tools used to explore alcoholism, dependency, and drug addiction beyond theory and training.

Filling in the missing gaps of knowledge was a self-appointed personal journey of exploring several disciplines. Harvesting the information came from probing the minds of colleagues, social workers, and clinicians, while interacting with experts and professionals in their respective fields. Those learning moments were priceless. I am eternally grateful for the exposure to a different side of the human equation beyond what was read, studied, and researched.

It was certainly an internal and personal struggle, having to witness the realities of others, who were engaged in alcohol abuse and drug addictive behaviors over the decades. Although the abuses were recognized by the abusers, most were fighting their demons with the best tools at their disposal, internal strength and willpower. However, willpower was not enough. Their expressed goal was to live independently of the need to use and subsequently abuse substances. I became a spectator to the struggle and ravages of abuse and its fruits.

For the great majority of those depicted herein, internal strength and willpower were not adequate to transition from, and become independent of structured rehabilitation programs. Their struggle seemed to have no end, as was their involvement with varying kinds of rehabilitation programs. It was a conundrum spinning them in an endless circle as time went by.

Others, who vocally rationalized or displaced their behaviors, became the thorn that reminded the observer not to infer or to advocate or to analyze the indulgences and behaviors of others. Remaining the observer called to attention the saying just live and let live, and pass no judgment. Be neutral to the nuances. The non-judgmental stand, as the saying goes, "don't judge me".

Just being an observer, while enforcing agency mandates, and advocating for clients, became difficult exercises in remaining nonjudgmental and empathic. Seeing blatant violations unfolding without voicing disapproval, not because you can't, but the penalties for recording a simple violation carried lengthy doses of continued agency involvement in client's lives. At the same time, struggling with the human instinct to extend a hand to those appealing for help beyond agency mandates was exasperating.

It was indeed a quandary just being human and confined not to think beyond the parameters of federal, state, and city regulations. Just because of agency stipulations, and adhering to the bureaucratic process, extending help and being flexible enough to ease the tensions of the addict and alcoholic seemed contradictory. One was caught in the bind of being human in an environment that flourished with conferences. These meetings were held to rehash the known issues of their client population and to satisfy their need for continued financing.

Verbal clashes were common with superiors, holding steadfast to written rules, and never giving consideration or flexibility on simple issues like visitation with a client before the officially required working hours. Inflexibility, Rules are Rules! It was simply an organization functioning in the absence of an informal concept of managing to maximize efficiency. Efficiency lay dormant and was stifled by the chain of command requirement that all must adhere to in social work practice.

Despite the difficulties and challenges of working with this population, the exposure, learning something new each day, kindled the fire for further inquiry into alcoholism specifically. It was this sense of inquiry that propelled the urge to acquire and develop another skill; listening carefully to unlock the doors for an understanding of the quagmire faced by those struggling with alcoholism and drug addiction.

INTRODUCTION

A larger number of those mentioned herein were engaged in numerous rehabilitation programs for an average of 10 years. Most were able to remain engaged in rehabilitation by traversing one program over another to remain relevant in seeking assistance. A few were at different phases of rehabilitation for over 20 years.

Traversing rehabilitation programs had become the norm throughout the lives of these individuals, which suggested that seeking help was the only path for them in their struggle to survive. Some referred to this modality as the "revolving door".

A few functional alcoholics and drug addicts stopped participating in any rehabilitative programs. However, on occasion, these individuals would deliberately become engaged in some form of an approved program, with the direct purpose to gain access either to cash funding, housing, or to maintain federal disability insurance gains. They understood what to do, and when. It was their human instinct to survive and by any means necessary, they did what they needed to do.

These individuals, far from being incapable of addressing some of their immediate needs, contributed, in whatever way opportunity presented. Despite their abilities, however limited, most voluntarily choose to have an advocate, such as a caseworker, to navigate the many levels of bureaucratic contingencies, when seeking assistance. In other words, this group implicitly demanded help because of their knowledge of federal mandates for granting assistance.

These functional abusers understood requirements, violations, and sanctions for failure to comply with directives coming from judges. Yet their ingrained acclamation, "I'm in recovery", became the banner that provided the vehicle for violations. In addition, this banner became reinforced with the theme, "I'm only human" as the shield. Preceding any engagement, clients prattled, "I'm in recovery", to call to attention their efforts at rehabilitation and by extension to seek empathy and assistance.

A majority, because they were taught that relapse does occur and can happen, felt entitled to violate as part of the recovery process. Since they are human and susceptible to all things human, this acceptance of intrinsic faults in psyche by addicts and alcoholics, and supported by clinicians, gave free acceptance that violations must be treated with verbal reprimands and are allowed to go without real penalty.

Coupled with this approach, social thinkers, and those in the helping professions are adherents who subscribe to the old saying, "it is better to save one life, no matter what the costs". Here we see the advocates for change trapping themselves into rewarding inappropriate behaviors because of the adage of their profession.

Because the phrase, "I'm human", acknowledges fault in the psyche, and relapse is taught as part of the healing process which leads to recovery, abusers continue to use these phrases while seeking assistance. In the colloquial style, it is called "making the system work for you" while "playing the system". It is simply taking advantage of federal and legal entitlement.

It should be pointed out a small percentage of alcoholics and drug addicts with whom I came in contact, were MICA -mentally ill chemical abuser- patients under psychiatric care and supervision. Of interest, most clients adhered to requirements and stipulations and did not make demands which infered "gaming the system".

No attempt is made herein, to attack or label programs as failures, or to infer that counseling or therapy sessions are not helpful in the process of recovery. Rather, what had been observed is that a greater sector of the alcoholic and drug addicted populations, who were involved in rehabilitative efforts, were using programs as a means to survive their daily challenges and stressful effects from the substances they used. I term this involvement as perfunctory participation. There are numerous studies and articles which suggest that support programs, similar to [4]Alcoholics Anonymous and [5]Narcotics Anonymous, are marginally effective, with first year relapse rates being rather high, which corroborates the "going through the motions" of participation.

We must also recognize the importance of immersed counseling engagement, which addresses the effects of abandonment emanating from abuse of substances. One of the most vocal spokespersons on the subject of abandonment is Judge Mathis. I will speak about his contributions to the issue of abandonment.

We all know the will to change is personal and challenging, and cannot be dictated by anyone or institution. We also know that humans are granted intellect, regardless of depth or its application, while cognitive ability is yet to be determined beyond the clinical setting. Since intellect exists, clients with limitations are able to make decisions, but fail to implement the decision in their best interest. Why is this taking place?

With that in mind, new thinking and approaches have to be examined. There needs to be a way to move forward for those in the dragon clutches of dependency and abuse of licit and illicit substances. Both substances will be discussed.

The focus of this work is another look at the struggles of alcoholics and drug abusers, and their difficulties at breaking the habit. It looks at the enablers, who in good faith, are caught in the clutches of advocacy and mandates for compliance. The world of those afflicted is herein presented by an onlooker who was filled with questions, despite a theoretical understanding. It takes the reader on a trip into the world and struggles of the abusers. I was looking, not only at the by-products of their addiction and dependencies, but for an understanding that remained hidden in valid clinical explanations.

Yet there was a missing link in all explanations. In my search, a connection was made which yielded further explanation. It was hidden in the physiology of the afflicted population. This will be explored.

The transition from legal prescription pain killers to heroin will be looked at in the context of New York City. Marijuana will be talked about in another light, reflecting the Zeitgeist of the times we live in.

ABANDONMENT

Abandonment and its bi-product, as seen in troubled youth, needs to be spelt out clearly, and as such, I chose a personality who exemplifies the latter and has shared his life in a public manner. Judge Greg Mathis is that person who has demonstrated that, "there's no adversity that one cannot pick themselves up from" and become successful. A little background is needed.

[6]Judge Mathis, according to a documentary on his life, was brought up in one of the worst housing projects in Detroit, Michigan, where his entire environment was inundated with heroin dealers, gangs, social misfits, absentee fathers, teenage pregnancy, failing schools and poor health facilities. Before age 17, he was a gang member, heroin dealer, and spent stints in juvenile detention numerous times. An ultimatum by a judge to either get a G.E.D (general equivalence diploma) for high school completion or go to jail coupled with a promise to his dying mother to turn his life around, were the deciding factors that influenced meaningful CHANGE in his life.

Because of Judge Greg Mathis' intimacy with past negative experiences, he has been speaking about abandonment for years by using his popular shows as the platform to expose and bring this serious issue to the forefront. As a retired Supreme Court Judge of [7] Michigan's 36th District Court, he incorporated true life stories into his show. The Judge is known to have publicly reprimanded defendants and respondents for negatively affecting the future of their children due to abandonment, resulting from alcohol and drug addiction.

According to Judge Mathis, when we talk of abandonment by the alcoholic or drug addict, we are talking of abandonment of everything: self, family, love ones, children, job, and career. The judge was quick to point out that abandonment is not confined or dominant only in the substance abusing population, but that it affects the general population with damaging results.

Not only does abandonment affect the abusers immediate world, it reaches far into the general population, affecting everything. Employers must replace the abuser, healthcare costs are absorbed, government agencies become overwhelmed, etc. For the abuser, all that matters is their next high.

Just for a moment, picture an alcoholic who gets up late in the night and needs a drink badly. His hands are beginning to shake but he says to himself, "I'm in control." An inner voice convinces him to wait until 8:30am when the liquor store opens. He gets back into bed, but his eyes cannot close. He stares at the huge, aged, Roman numeral faced clock perched on the old wooden dresser at the foot of the bed. A gift from his in-laws some fifteen years ago to remind him that Time is everything, and at all times. It is 11:30pm, almost closing time for most liquor stores. The thought crosses his mind to forgo the alcohol and get busy with his spouse who does not have an assignment at the local hospital for the next two days.

She came into the bedroom earlier in the evening with a tantalizing twitch in her eyes. She gleefully announced, and with a sigh of relief, that she will be home for the next two days and free of patient care. She went to the upper floor to put their daughter to sleep. She wants to get busy with him.

His thought of an intimate evening with his spouse became secondary, as he remained fixated on the clock; it is almost midnight. He continues to stare into space as he ponders his choices of getting busy with his woman or running out to search for an open liquor store. The internal debate continues. It is getting close for all neighborhood liquor stores to end their day's business.

He spontaneously jumps out of his bed. He is discombobulated because time is running out, and stores are closing, and he needs a drink; a beer is not going to do it.

He is scrambling to get his clothing on. He is searching for his door keys. His eyes are on the clock as he rushes out of the apartment and speedily walks to his car. He suddenly realizes that he parked his car earlier in the evening three blocks away to guarantee not getting a parking ticket in the morning. He turns around and begins running towards his car in the opposite direction. He hastily jumps into the driver's seat and speeds away on his journey to the liquor store.

He is out of breath and his nerves are on edge as he arrives at the liquor store, but it is closed. Decisions have to be made. He needs to get to the next liquor store a mile away. He jumps back into the drivers' seat and drops his right foot heavily on the gas pedal bringing a screeching sound to the silent air; it is midnight. In the far distance, the flashing neon lights of the liquor store are on, yet seems to be disappearing. He is in a hurry and the car seems not to be moving fast enough. Time is of essence and the clock is running out.

What a relief, the store is still open. He hastily parks the vehicle at the fire hydrant and rushes to the store. The door is locked and a cross bar is in place. He shakes the door a second time in disbelief, motioning to an employee to open the door, but is ignored. People are still mingling in the store and making purchases. He tries again to get attention by throwing a stone at the door. He is ignored by everyone. This cannot be happening! Big John guards the exit. No one enters.

He needs a drink, desperately! He slowly walks back to his car shaking his head in disbelief. All liquor stores in the neighborhood are closed. It is now past midnight. He disappointedly enters his car. He drops into the driver's seat with the frustration of a beaten prize fighter. He remains motionless while contemplating his next move. The ringing of his cell phone disturbs him. "What, what?" he responds in an angry tone. "You should have gone to the store earlier to buy the baby's food, and now you want me to go looking for baby food now? You've got to be kidding". His yelling into the cell phone continues as his frustration mounts.

He utters to himself, "I'm trying to get a taste right now and this woman is tasking me about baby food, I can't believe this at this time." He looks at the store once more in disbelief. Then suddenly he comes alive as he notices a friend exiting the store with two bags filled with spirits. He spontaneously jumps out of his seat, leaving the door open as he rushes across the street. "Basil, what's up?" His mind is only on a taste of liquor. Basil has the answer and the solution to his anxiety.

"Everything is good. We're having a birthday party tomorrow night, so I decided to pick up the liquor now", Basil responded. "Do me favor, I'm really in a jam," he stated. "How can I help you, brother?" Basil asked. "I need a taste, see my hand is shaking, the store closed on me, them m-----f-----s", he irritatingly complained. "I just bought this for the party tomorrow", Basil informed him. "Look, do me a favor, I'll double the price", he begged. "I need this shit for the party, plus how am I going to replace the liquor? Girlfriend counts everything.", Basil said. "I'll give you $50 for that bottle of light rum you have in the bag.", pleaded the alcoholic. "You got it.", Basil replied, acquiescing to his buddy.

Judge Mathis stated, "Treatment is necessary to explain and to bring to light the toll of devastation beyond the abuser's recognition." Profound indeed!

To the reader, take the bull by the horn, despite resistance, and seek treatment for those afflicted with the ills of alcoholism or drug abuse.

On a hot summer day, years ago, I made face-to-face contact with the parents of two school aged children.

Both birth parents were alleged to be using heroin on a regular basis, which resulted in the neglect of their two young children, aged seven and nine. It was their first meeting with personnel from Children Services.

Tanya and Boris, biological parents, as I would refer to them, were both professionals in their respective fields. Tanya, a pediatric dentist, who surrendered and subsequently lost her license to practice, was charming and introduced herself with the refinement of an English lady brought up in the country side not far from [8] Guildford Castle –which I read about in my youth.

Boris, a successful stock broker, who was forced to tender his resignation and surrender his broker's license to the [9] Security & Exchange Commission, was sharp, direct, and calculating. He spoke with the air of authority, as would be expected by someone who had worked on Wall Street, and mingled in the bowels of the financial world during Michael Milken and Ivan Bosky's tenure on Wall Street. Boris was "up there", using the street vernacular, with the so-called fat cats and power brokers of Wall Street.

In the 1990s, Michael Milken developed, with others, the market for high-yield bonds; junk bonds. He was jailed for manipulations of stocks and grading of bonds, among other things, leading to the financial collapse on Wall Street. Milken became the American billionaire and philanthropist who heads the [10] Milken Family Foundation to support medical research and education and founded the Prostate Cancer Foundation.

Life for Boris and Tanya changed dramatically. Both were now physically beaten, and paid very little attention to their appearances. Boris sported a tangled lump of hair protruding from his chin that had a semblance of a beard. Tanya gained weight and developed a pear shaped body that contradicted her belief in the sculpted body shape for the progressive woman.

Boris and Tanya had lost their careers and were tarnished in their respective fields. Savings had been depleted. Credit cards surrendered. Having dinner out of the home was now beyond the family's reach. Homes they had in the community and the country house were in foreclosure. Children were attending public school and were no longer driven to school in either parent's Mercedes or BMW, but accompanied to school by a caring neighbor whenever either parent was too "out of it"; as the parents were described by collateral sources. Boris was dependent on alcohol, and Tanya was addicted to heroin.

Tanya detailed working as a pediatric dentist for 10 years at one of the leading teaching hospitals. A promising career with fellowships and access to breaking technology awaited her in her chosen field and specialty; success at every venture was almost guaranteed. She mingled with the upwardly mobile professionals and freshly minted medical colleagues. "Life was good", as Tanya described her early years as a professional. As Tanya recalled, all the physical trappings and well connected associates in her life provided the fuel she needed to rapidly advance her career. She was chasing a dream.

Tanya was introduced to heroin involuntarily by a clinical associate who was already addicted. Tanya smoked marijuana daily, as she did since her undergraduate days, but it was a different experience smoking a mixture of heroin and Marijuana. It transcended what she was accustomed to over the years. Her first introduction to heroin took place when her high grade marijuana, which she smoked on a regular basis, was laced with heroin. It became an accidental beginning to a continuous journey without an end!

As I engaged Tanya, she fidgeted, yet exhibited perkiness when reflecting on her past intimacy with heroin. She spoke in a disjointed manner as she described her journey with heroin which began with a "laced joint". That "first hit", as she recalled the first time she smoked heroin, was the "high of all highs", and the best of anything she had smoked so far. Tanya's first hit was the beginning of a long journey propelled by an unquenchable thirst for the next high. She needed this dangerous combination at any cost; indeed, it did cost her. For Tanya, it became "chasing the high"; always wanting a lasting euphoria from a waning intoxicant.

Tanya wanted more; she compromised for more.

Within a few months, Tanya, who was introduced to heroin involuntarily, began habitually snorting bags of heroin daily. In the morning before leaving for work to provide dental care for children, she snorted a bag. On her lunch breaks, a booster dose was the routine. She became a slave to the drug. She understood its dangers as a clinician, yet felt in control. She did not see addiction or dependency as having relevance in her life.

While under the influence, Tanya was blind to her environment; oblivious to everything important. What she did not know was that her associates were beginning to notice changes in her work attitude and decorum. Associates gossiped, as complaints were made to supervisors about her seeming indifference for quality of work; her failure to appear at work without a valid explanation; and most of all, parents were complaining about her failure to review x-rays and extracting a wrong tooth. She was falling down a rabbit hole. Associates and peers came to her rescue.

Tanya was offered intervention, but became belligerent and verbally obnoxious to all within the circle of professionals with whom she associated on a daily basis. A leave of absence for a few months, not to seek rehabilitation, but to be away from the work environment, to contemplate her next move; either private practice or a new assignment, was what she offered.

She felt in control of everything. However, she was about to find out she could not control the habit which was about to raise its ugly head, leading her into the valley of lost souls. Tanya headed in that direction very quickly. Her savings were dwindling as her appetite for drugs became insatiable. As she continued snorting, quantities grew larger, more frequent, and costly. Her habit progressed quickly, transitioning to regular injections.

A year later, she was still on extended leave from work. She had numerous hospitalizations for hepatitis and an overdose of heroin, which caused her to remain on a respirator until I got the call of her demise. She abandoned her children, career, family, and herself to the end.

Another contact I made over the years in a social setting makes the point of abandonment in another way that exemplifies the effects of alcohol.

A young male, whom I will refer to as Dennis, was introduced to me at a social gathering to celebrate a new component in computer design. Dennis appeared to be a very cordial and jovial individual with a charming and dynamic personality. He was a computer engineer with an Ivy League education. These institutions were his homes and incubators for robotics engineering, theory, and application.

I recall Dennis dressed in loafers, boat shoes to be specific, that complimented his burgundy bowtie. His attire suggested a time when the Beach Boys were popular. He carried an air of a nerd in isolation as he fiddled with a gadget in his hand. However, his glasses revealed another side of his genius; he was able to see in two directions at the same time (front and back). He built a tiny pair of mirrors into his glasses. Dennis was different and likable.

At the gathering, Dennis mingled freely with all the invitees, moving from one group to another with precision, while allocating communication time with each group sparingly. Dennis always thought of things in a logical progression. He was charming, cordial, and prudent. There was always spontaneity about him that accompanied his reflexive smile when acknowledging the not so important guests. He went from one group to another. Each encounter that he made, prior to engaging in discussion of a new product, was preceded by a toast of alcohol. He was toasting everyone with a freshly poured drink in his hand.

From where I stood, the view was clear enough for me to see the attendees and Dennis as he mingled. Dennis had already toasted six groups; it was his custom to have a drink with everyone in the room. For Dennis, each group required a fresh drink. There were about 12 groups, conversing as they waited for Dennis to make his way through the room. Dennis was referred to by most colleagues as "the man" who made the difference with an introduction of a new product into the market place. Dennis was described by others as, "the symbol of success" and a "true ladies' man".

His wife expressed her concerns for his progression; he was taking a few shots of alcohol before breakfast every morning. This behavior was nothing new; it had been going on for several years. During the workweek, he would repeat the same performance upon his arrival home. The weekends were nothing more than marathons of alcohol indulgence, where excessive inebriation became a badge of honor. He termed his weekend binging with associates as "reasoning sessions", just like Plato's dialogue in his symposium on soul mates.

Dennis did not assist with anything in the home beyond writing the checks for monthly expenses. If there was a need to fix an electric socket or do minor plumbing he took a leave of absence from the home. After all, chores like these were challenges, and he considered them not in his domain of expertise. Rather, Dennis would summon a contractor to ensure the job was professionally done. Like most men, he disliked shopping, but whenever he had to accompany his spouse to the supermarket, a few drinks always preceded his decision to leave home, if at all. On a number of occasions, even if there was an emergency, it became a futile exercise trying to extricate him from home before he had his REQUIRED number of drinks. He remained committed to only one thing that matters- ALCOHOL! His sudden death from a heart attack with liver complications was the product of his habit.

Dennis, a promising athlete during his high school and college days, was home bound and attached to the bottle. He would spend hour after hour fixated on the television screen ostensibly viewing the news or sports, but in reality, he was DRINKING! It was as if he were enjoying tea at all times. He remained in the same spot on the sofa and took occasional breaks to either use the bathroom or fill his glass with ice cubes. You knew when the effects of alcohol kicked in- he would immediately begin to do the waltz by himself to music he could hear from the adjacent apartment. This became his modus operandi.

Dennis subsequently developed liver complications and was placed on dialysis. Nevertheless, he continued drinking moderately; he felt himself completely unable to stop. He wanted to end alcohol's dominance.

Dennis was separated from his spouse after his last hospitalization at a trauma center in another state. Upon his discharge from the hospital, he headed to his favorite bar for a few drinks, as usual. He drank as he was accustomed to, whenever he felt the urge. The need to drink was always there. He was a regular at the local tavern where he was greeted and acknowledged by everyone whenever he arrived. He always left the tavern after having his fill and would walk briskly to the subway to begin the journey home.

An old associate of mine recalled, witnessing an incident years ago, while standing on the uptown platform of the subway. According to him, he saw a black male tumbling down a few flights of stairs and landing on the platform encased in a long black trench coat. As he focused, his vision on the fallen body he noticed the figure struggling to get up while desperately trying to compose himself as he reached for an unknown object. As he struggled to rise, he staggered into a pole, which gave him the support he needed to avoid falling again. His clothing was torn and exposed a broken and bloody right arm. Bruises were on his knees, back, right side of his face and shoulder. It was Dennis. My associate could not render any assistance. They were standing on opposite platforms as their respective trains approached.

He was torn, bruised, bloody, and in pain. Yet, he defied logic that dictated seeking medical intervention. He continued to his destination while avoiding any eye contact with the public; he was embarrassed. He entered the subway car looking like a wild alley mutt. Most riders gave a quick glance at him and shook their heads in disgust.

Dennis was incoherent and inebriated. The pungent aroma of alcohol permeated the stuffy air of the subway platform and in the car. He drew sideways looks and hushed whispers from riders. Nevertheless, he continued his way. It was a struggle for him to stand upright without staggering from side to side. He navigated between the crowds of people from one train to a connecting line. Years later, Dennis revealed to me that he was totally "out of it" and could not recall getting home that particular night. He knew he broke his arm that night, NOTHING MORE!

According to Dennis, when he arrived home that night he was shunned and castigated by his better half, as she had done in the past, but with an air of disgust and purpose in her threats to leave him. She did not look at him but remained transfixed on the television in the bedroom. She vented her frustrations above the blaring tv, angrily changing channels. She was exasperated! There was no other way to reach him.

His being drunk was commonplace now. She had warned him his drinking made her numb to his complaints. Dennis habitually blamed the demands of his job as the primary reason for his drinking. BUT, a broken arm and bruises about his body, due to excessive drinking was beyond her comprehension!

On a prior occasion, after he collapsed on the kitchen floor, his wife shouted at the top of her lungs, "I've had it with you and your drinking!" She was at her wits end but had no alternative due to her reliance on him for financial support. She felt trapped without any alternative.

As was his routine, Dennis would make his way into the kitchen in search of food as soon as he arrived home after drinking. On the occasion when a meal was prepared, and this was rare, he would help himself to a small portion to satisfy his need for sustenance. Dennis NEEDED another drink. He drank FAR more than he ate.

He apologized numerous times to his wife, even promising to drink moderately. He even inferred intervention would be considered, if necessary, to keep the relationship going. "Yea, right" was her standard response to his apologies and promises. The apologies were nothing new, having become routine long ago. She described his behavior as "disturbing and troubling". He was estranged from his wife for 5 years because of his excessive drinking. His marriage eventually ended in divorce.

Dennis was apart from his woman of 20 years, but failed to recognize the fracture in their relationship. She was only tolerating him because of her current circumstances, and the need to have a residence. She was dependent on Dennis financially, and he knew she had minimal resources to support herself. As a former cocaine abuser, clean for over ten years, she understood Dennis' struggle, but not his propensity to consume large volumes of alcohol. She referred to alcohol as the devil in a bottle, verbalizing her refusal to engage the devil. She spoke like an evangelist when alcohol was the subject.

Not only was Dennis' relationship on shaky ground, steadily drifting apart, but the relationship with his daughter had become perfunctory. Her visits with him were waning and sporadic. Most contact was done by telephone, direct and short. She hated the thought of having a discussion with him because she believed his thinking was driven by alcohol. She complained continuously about her inability to have a meaningful conversation with him because he was always drunk. She was convinced his drinking was unmanageable. Still, she continued trying to make sense of her father's behavior.

Years ago, she made her appeal. She requested that we – friends-take care of her father, as she motioned to his better half on her way out the apartment. There was a look of displeasure on her face.

Dennis had been drinking excessively since the birth of his daughter, and progressed to the point where he was only able to associate with friends when alcohol was present. If he knew he would be attending a dry function, no alcohol, he wouldn't leave home until he consumed his fill.

He lost his driver's license, after being arrested, jailed, and convicted for driving while intoxicated. He was mandated to alcohol rehabilitation for 18 months and DMV classes every Saturday for a few months. Dennis attended rehabilitation and DMV classes, while expressing trepidation at the thought of rehabilitation. He graduated from both programs after, according to him, "going through the motions", during all phases of treatment.

Thank you JESUS! It resounded by all family members when the news got out that Dennis was mandated to rehabilitation. Everyone thought that this incident was the wakeup call for him to detox and become free of alcohol. Friends mobilized in their support of him while he attended an out-patient alcohol program.

Despite the their strong support, he was indifferent to all who supported him while in rehabilitation. He continued drinking, alienating everyone in his immediate circle. Everyone tried to engage him in conversation, hoping for an admission his alcohol abuse was a problem. He was simply going through the motions, as he often stated, to be freed of the judicial system and going to prison.

Dennis drank throughout his months of rehabilitation and met with his counselor twice each week. He never consumed alcohol 24 hours preceding any contact and session with his counselor. He successfully kept within the range for non- detection of alcohol in his system whenever he was tested. He was fully aware of what he was doing.

When Dennis was questioned about his excessive drinking, his continued response remained the same. I recall on one occasion, he rationalized his drinking by mentioning the inevitable that we all face-death. He believed that it is better to enjoy a drink while alive because the ultimate end to existence is guaranteed. It was his standard response to anyone probing into his excessive drinking.

A friend, who was visiting him after a long absence, stated to Dennis bluntly, "Listen, it's the family, you, and the quality of your existence that matters!" He was angry and disappointed at Dennis' continued response when someone questioned him on his ongoing indulgence of alcohol.

Once again, he repeated the standard statement about his father, who drank heavily, and lived until he was ninety four. His grandmother, who lived until she was one hundred years old, drank a pint every week. This evidence of longevity, despite drinking, became proof and ammunition to rationalize his drinking and to avoid talking about the physical, emotional, and social impact his drinking has had on his relationships over the years. He refused to see his excessive indulgence as a dependency and disorder that needed to be addressed.

After presenting such rationalization to avoid any further discussion on any topic of excessive drinking, alcoholism, or dependency, Dennis went to the kitchen. He returned with a cup in hand, sipping a combination of rum and beer. Dennis had abandoned everyone for his fill. He relegated all concepts taught during his sojourn in rehabilitation to the abyss, and accepted his status as an alcoholic.

He had a kidney transplant and appeared to be doing moderately well the last time we made contact. At that time, he appeared to be older than his chronological age. His stomach was distended; he complained often about digestive problems and was seeing his gastroenterologist like clock- work for the same ongoing problems. He was unable to walk a few blocks because his legs were discolored and swollen from water retention and circulatory problems. Yet, he continued to drink and remain a fixture on his sofa, where the outlines of his body markings were clearly visible. I wished him well.

Many months later I read in the local news his lifeless body was found in his favorite spot, the television replaying an old John Wayne movie.

A burly person, whom I met decades ago, was a prosecutor with a promising future in law and politics. He was very similar to Dennis in his response to excessive drinking. He always stated and rationalized his behavior as being genetic, and as such, predisposed him to drink alcohol excessively. However, alcohol was not the major issue affecting his life, cocaine was the monster.

Cocaine became the catalyst for all his underlying problems. Yet his propensity to consume volumes of alcohol the night before trying cases was astounding and incomprehensible. He would drink throughout case preparation, just as one consumes water after a long dehydrating sprint. He was known as someone who could hold his liquor "like a man", while masking and keeping the "BIG C", as he called it, "at bay" and "manageable", as he recollected. At least he thought so, but onlookers and colleagues had other opinions.

He was the son of a bi-racial mother, who disliked being identified in racial terms. She worked as a social worker in the bowels of some of the worst housing projects in the United States for three decades. His Caucasian father worked as a medical doctor in several inner city communities for three decades. It was during his practice he began sharing himself with two women in adjacent states twenty miles apart.

Frank, a product of this union, stood out in an incongruous manner that defined him from those in the community; he looked white in a sea of black faces but defined himself as bi-racial and never as black. He stuck to his argument that he would not be defined by anyone but himself. He believed that it was a disingenuous label to attach to anyone. He felt better being labeled with the inclusiveness of both contributors to his birth, and its distinctiveness of making him a bi-racial person or as President Barack Obama referred to himself as a "mutt" on November 06, 2008. After everything is said and done, race does not exist in biology- a fact.

Despite being in a community that was defined by its poverty and lack of paternal involvement, he escaped participating in the negative attributes of a community in decline, while maintaining an intimacy with the nuances of everyday life. He enjoyed the privilege of being the only child, and was afforded the opportunity to attend selective and exclusive boarding schools while living in the United States, while holding duo-citizenship with a Latin nation. Life was good for him.

Frank, as most referred to him for his resentment for fiction, graduated from a prestigious university and was valedictorian when he graduated from law school in Europe. When he returned home, on his first try he passed the bar examination and was admitted to practice in one of our largest states. According to Frank, he started to "dabble" with cocaine during his law school days, and developed an affinity quickly for the drug. Alcohol was another substance that came to him naturally because of his family background; everyone drank. According to him, all family members had a drink for everything that needed to be celebrated. It seemed that a celebration was taking place continuously.

However, cocaine was another indulgence that massaged his feelings, and was the ingredient that aided him through the stressful periods when he practiced law. According to him, a line or two of cocaine in the morning followed by a drink was all that was needed for him to begin the day. It became his routine. However, he was at the top of his game, and maintained the domineering personality he needed to win.

As a top prosecutor, he was always in the spotlight and under scrutiny. He was handling a very demanding case load of more than 100. The late hours at night and extended time spent in the law library, started to take its toll on his sleeping habits. He did not have time for the gym, like early in his career. It was all work and he was in a hurry to climb the ladder to success. The pressures of the job were beginning to manifest themselves in many ways. He was losing weight and ate infrequently.

Colleagues and others in the legal profession were beginning to take notice of changes in his approach in case preparation for trials. Warnings from superiors of his decorum meant little. He was taking on a greater case load and winning while indulging more often. All that mattered to him was winning at all cost.

Over the course of a year, he was counseled by senior staff members to seek intervention. It was even proposed that he enter an in-patient facility for rehabilitation. He was assured that there would be no recriminations or entries made in his employment, or in his portfolio, to reflect a history or any history of substance abuse. He was offered a leave of absence for one year with full salary. To add assurance of his status, he was also promised that he would not be demoted or relegated to a junior position in the district attorney's office upon his return from drug rehabilitation. Everything was in his hands to progress successfully.

He recalled going crazy at the thought of someone suggesting to him to enter an in-patient rehabilitation facility, and making use of the psychiatric help that he needed to understand his addiction and dependency. He was furious and locked into his own thinking, but beneath the façade, he was ashamed to admit that he had an addiction and was dependent on alcohol. He also convinced himself, despite knowing the personal toll both issues demanded from him on an ongoing basis, that he was in control of his life. His rationalization was that alcoholism came with the family genes that needed to be fed.

He became very resistant to any advice, which treaded upon his indulgences. Anyone who expressed an opinion on the subject of addiction and dependency, were immediately dumped into the wastebasket of persons who, according to him, "need to mind their own business". He rejected seeking help because he thought that he was in control of his cocaine intake. He was not in control.

The ultimate occurred- fired and subsequently disbarred. He became an outcast, and was relegated by associates and family members to the wastebasket of human suffering brought about by his addiction. He was unable to find employment in the legal profession or apply for any positions that would unearth his negative history.

On our last contact, a few years ago, preceding his killing, he was afflicted with arthritis in his hips and right shoulder and was diabetic. Because of his disabilities and paucity of finances, life became difficult just living above the margins, yet he persisted in making the best of whatever was presented to him, as he remained in a rent subsidized apartment. As a former prosecutor, he was providing free legal advice to alcoholics and other substance abusers who made a voluntary contribution for his assistance. The fees he collected for his services and social security disability benefits afforded him the opportunity to maintain his decency. He has been substance free for the past 5 years. He severed his long relationship with all forms of structured rehabilitation programs, and cemented a relationship with a Higher Power. Frank remained committed to a drug free existence.

On our last visit several years ago, he was coherent, clean, and well dressed. It was a transformation, which he confirmed when he emphatically declared his drug free status. He was clean. Two weeks later, it was reported in the local media that he held up at gun point and shot to death in the left temple.

THE PROCESS

The accountings that follow are from observations, conversations with former clients and colleagues, statements from professionals in their respective fields, anecdotes, and professional journals. From these sources, the author relays the major issues affecting abusers of substances.

The impact of substance abuse on their lives and extended families members, despite voluntarily and involuntary involvement with rehabilitation programs, are brought to light herein. It is their journey.

However, presenting their journey demanded not only observation but also keen insight into their lives. At the same time, trying to have a good working understanding of the alcoholic and drug addicted populations became not only a challenge that needed to be examined, but also tolerance of immense proportion.

The challenge was to discover with specificity within the conundrum of opinions coming from every expert in their respective field, and to have purpose in trying to understand what propels their addiction and dependency. However, understanding the complexities of alcoholism and drug addiction had its demands and prerequisites for the task ahead.

Taking graduate courses in counseling techniques while digging into research materials, and participating in forums, provided a good framework to begin the process of unraveling theory. Integrating the concepts of counseling, while working with the two populations, became the battle ground of understanding. Yet, something seemed to be missing in the approaches or focus towards sobriety and substance free existence for the population at hand.

However, it appeared both populations had a commonality, beyond dependency or addiction, which kept the abuser functional. Functional in the sense that they were all doing what was necessary for their basic survival. Some, like John, have reported to me, survival methods that guaranteed good quality food and free of charge, on a daily basis.

John, not his true name and whose true name remains a mystery, was a planner, organizer, and tactician, all wrapped up in one.

John detailed to me his weekly plans for food, and voluntarily provided the locations where donations were coming from churches, restaurants, and pantries. Yet, he was not forthcoming with information on upscale restaurants in that part of the city; he kept it a secret, because his appetite was now acclimated to the different cultural foods at his disposal.

He knew, yet made written notations regarding the day and time when seafood dishes, which were not sold, and could not be left over for the next day, would be disposed. All notations regarding these establishments were placed in a manila folder to be retrieved when needed. Yet, he made daily checks in the folder, to be assured that his memory of all events past and present, were retained in his brain. John had a phobia of inheriting the Alzheimer syndrome that had affected several family members.

John was very cordial, and managed over time, to befriend the owners of some upscale establishments. He was treated like a needed entity that presented no problem and even arranged to receive cooked and unsold food before it was discarded late at night. Because of his cordiality, pleasantness, and use of the English language, he had an aura that impelled one to offer assistance. One could not help but extending that helping hand to John.

A visit to his studio apartment provided some insight into his functioning, organizing, and planning skills. Such were the prerequisites for surviving the bowels of a housing project known for spontaneous violence incidents for minor incidents of disagreements over the years. This was a place of abode in hell, and fit for the comfort of the devil and his cohorts.

On the kitchen wall adjacent to a large refrigerator, were stick-on pieces of paper, with the names of restaurants written on the top, and at the bottom the scheduled times for food disposal. He also scribbled the type of food discarded and on what days of the week. John had this arrangement done in such a way that allowed him to eat a different dish every day of the week. Seafood dishes and prime steaks days were highlighted in green.

The stunner came when I noticed several sheets of paper pasted on another wall in the kitchen. The white wall had a collage of addresses, telephone numbers, and schedules for churches and pantries where food was served free on a daily basis. Notations were made in red next to the names of organizations, which, according to John, "rubbed me the wrong way", relegating them to last preference when seeking assistance. John ensured food was not an issue for him; neither should it be an issue for those in need. He shared his food with everyone.

Substance abusers like John, were also creative in their approaches for evading detection of illicit substances or alcohol by clinicians. He created a cottage industry in procuring and selling urines, female and male, that were free of illicit substances. John even amassed a list of regular customers, who submitted to so-called random testing, that lacked proper supervision to ensure accuracy and competence. Alcoholics and drug addicts are good researchers for programs that are lenient and locked into the concept of only being human, because such programs allow the client not to be sanctioned either financially or punitively for positive drug samples. Abusers are counseled on the ramifications of their actions, but remember such behaviors amplify the phrase, only being human, to explain behaviors.

Many substance abusers took advantage of additional assistance extended to them by clinicians, who became perfunctory in extending a helping hand. In many instances, clinicians became the enabler by allowing empathy to override punitive actions. These clinicians have inculcated into their lexicon that the actions of abusers are the result of only being human, and a positive result did not warrant punitive actions. Rather, the actions taken by these clinicians were focused on counseling, which addresses the implications of their continued submission of positive urine samples. Because clinicians are empathetic, it is only human for them to acquiesce to their client's pleas, by humanizing addiction and dependency to a level where tolerance shields the abuser from penalty.

It seemed the inculcation of the two phrases, "I'm only human." and "I'm in recovery.", became the abusers sword and shield into perpetuity. For them, these adages meant entitlement when seeking assistance, they should never be refused. It's time to look elsewhere for answers beyond the usual talk therapy, by incorporating medications to help free the alcoholic or addict.

Some of the findings that follow are corroborated by new research, while others are anecdotal. Relaying this material, which occurred over a twenty year period, without the aid of notes, would have been a conundrum.

Hearing the stories directly from the mouths of the functional substance abusers, was a test of tolerance, and at times, demanded a total role immersion into their world as it unfolded. At times, it meant joining the illusion, as it is referred to, gave a clearer insight into their lives. It also meant being physically present during their indulgences. Just being present during indulgences was difficult, and having to remain neutral while freeing the judgmental aspects of the human psyche was challenging. As an observer, the difficulty of learning to listen to the nuances of the voices was worth the effort of twenty years of work.

THE CRIES

In late 1999, Dolly, not her true name, but for some strange reason I associated her with a doll. Maybe because of her size or childlike behavior, her name remains with me as Dolly. I was exposed to her during the placement into foster care of her three children.

At first, she presented herself as a very obtuse person with a need for refinement. She was rough at the edges. Her speech was muffled and disjointed, as she spoke from one subject to another, and at times, completely incoherent. Her language shifted from Pidgin English to a Spanish dialect with abruptness.

Dolly, who wanted immediate attention, banged her hands on the counter of the front desk in the reception area, exclaiming: "Dam, who the hell has my children?" This was Dolly's way of introducing herself. "And, who are you and whom do you want to see?" inquired the security guard who was sitting behind the reception desk. "My three children that are what I'm talking about. Shit, they were illegally snatched and removed from my house, and I am going to sue the City, the Mayor, and the worker!" explained Dolly, "Who is your worker?" asked the guard. "How the hell am I supposed to know, he and the other prick took my children away yesterday: those sons of a bitches! I'm suing", Dolly, shouted. "Who is your worker?" the guard, once again, inquired in a very cordial manner. There was no response. Dolly was silent with a blank expression on her face that suggested a wondering mind lost in details. She seemed puzzled at the question and looked around with searching eyes as if in anticipation of a phantom to provide the correct answer. "Take a seat and I'll get some assistance for you," replied the guard.

Once again, she seemed lost at the guard's instruction to take a seat. She reflexively sat down, but with a level of apprehension that suggested an anachronistic event was about to take place, and was in the making. She had a penetrative expression on her face, inferring deep thought and that something was not quite clear in her mind. She shook her head in a negative manner and stated, "I can't believe this shit".

Dolly looked around with wandering eyes in a daze of involuntary inquiry. She crimped her forehead, but in an oddly complimenting way to a protruding chin, seeking attention. She shrugged her shoulder and motioned in an appealing manner for crowd support. She wanted to be heard by other clients who were seated in the waiting room. It was an appeal for solidarity from clients, who were waiting and restless in anticipation of news about their children, or actions taken by the court in their absence.

She knew from experience that most clients sitting in the waiting area were angry, and under stress from the agency's intervention into their personal lives. She was angrily directing all verbal assaults at representatives of the agency, and all persons in authority. Many harbored negative beliefs towards the agency for having taken their children into protective custody. Others, despite knowing that their past actions carried legal penalties, did not want to be lectured to for violations or to be directed to do what is in the best interest of their children and by extension for themselves. Dolly knew the environment well and how to gain attention.

Everyone seemed angry for some reason, but remained relatively calm and frozen in anticipation to hear their name being called. Body language spoke a million words of aggravation at the unknown, while verbal assaults were vindictive.

One young female kept grumbling about the decisions she made to remain involved in the lives of her children. The most inhuman decision she had to make, as a parent, was to surrender her children for protective reasons. This young woman was in an abusive and explosive relationship with her boyfriend, who was the father of both children. He also lived in the same household.

Everyone in the waiting area was angry at something or themselves, and was ready to explode. It was a charged and tense environment ticking slowly away.

Dolly knew exactly was she was doing and was ready to play the crowd by stoking their anger to gain approval. She looked carefully at those seated and with a façade of frustration on their faces, while thoughtfully priming her mind for additional ways to gain attention. Suddenly she exploded with verbal outbursts bordering on profanity and directed at the agency.

"Nigga, you better get me some help before war breaks out here, you people are playing with my children!" Dolly responded to the polite gesture from the guard, who moments earlier, offered her a seat in the waiting area.

A chorus of clients immediately chimed into an outburst of grunts, with undertones of profanity. Clients were angry and fidgeted incessantly to imply that there was an urgency elsewhere, which needed their immediate attention.

"Who the hell do they think they are?" asked a high pitched female voice, seemingly wrenched of displeasure for having to be in such a place of inconvenience.

"Always taking children for stupid shit", responded a black female, whose decorum implied that trouble lurks in the inside of the cirrostratus of her indulgence. She was boiling over with anger.

"Yea, they better take care of business or they would be speaking with my lawyer," stated another female whose speech was course and punctuated with a familiar Spanish idiom: pendejo, good for nothing, as she referred to agency workers. "B C W, I am tired of them. Always in people business." uttered another female client.

The public and those who have been involved with children services, refer to ACS as BCW. ACS (Administration for Children Services) was formerly known as Special Services for Children and preceding that, BCW (Bureau of Child Welfare), under the umbrella of the Department of Social Services. The latter morphed into its status, by charter, into a new entity in 1998 to continue to address the needs of children specifically. Child welfare workers received the new title of Child Protective Specialist on February 19, 1999. Nicholas Scoppetta was the Commissioner and Rudolph W. Giuliani was Mayor of New York City.

From the use of the acronym BCW (Bureau of Child Welfare), one could have easily assumed that the responder had a working knowledge or had prior involvement with Children Services, or been involved with the city agency. BCW did not represent, in the eyes of the poor and indigent, the theoretical mandate within its own self to address their needs.

The old acronym BCW, by reputation, presented fear to persons who were derelict in their responsibilities for providing care and supervision of children. BCW became known as the disrupter of families, as many poor and indigent persons referred to the agency, and whose only sins were being poor and lacking advocates to protect families from the intrusion by personnel from the aforementioned agency. Bluntly put, BCW was seen as the government's piranha that was used to destroy families.

The stains of BCW have remained indelible in the minds of the older generation, and for good reasons, and transposed itself into the newer generation with the same fear and hostility towards the agency now called ACS. The latter, although an advocate for families and children in particular, is still seen by many as an agency dictated by federal mandates for funding and supported by multi-layered bureaucrats and personnel in duplicitous position driven by unionism and nepotism. This perception continues despite efforts to change the agency in a humane manner.

"Yea, Special Services for Children, same shit! They have been messing with my family since I was a kid," stated a young woman who appeared to be in her early twenties. "Who is this BCW and Special Services for Children that you are talking about?" the question coming from an unknown male in the crowded waiting area.

The male who asked the question was waiting in a special area for a supervised visit with his children. The children were in placement due to neglect and abuse by their birth mother. Parents were estranged but remained in contact. It was his first involvement with this social services agency.

"Man where have you been? I have known these sons of bitches since I went into foster care when I was eight years old," stated another person. "They are all the same, only name changes with different workers and nothing more," replied a male who went asleep quickly after voicing his unsolicited opinion. "This agency has to go, always in people's business," stated another person, whose hands were filled with what appeared to be dispositional orders from the court, birth certificates, Medicaid cards, and other important documents.

"Now they call themselves the Administration for Children Services.", was the statement made by another person who joined the chorus of complainants. "Ain't that a bitch, what are they going to do for me now that they have my children?" stated a young woman who was tearing, while accusing the agency of not minding their own business.

Upon inquiry, it was learned that the young woman's children were removed because of physical abuse and neglect. She was suspected by her assigned caseworker, from the inhalation of fumes while visiting the family, that she was smoking marijuana while the children were in the home. She acknowledged that she was required to submit to drug screening, but failed to appear on the scheduled date and time to submit urine samples because of documented judicial issues in Family Court on the scheduled day for testing. She felt that the caseworker was unreasonable in not considering the unpredictable completion time of an ongoing hearing before scheduling her drug screening. She also complained about the inflexible nature of her assigned worker, whom she described as not "giving any slack" and sticking and going "by the book". "What the heck, if I smoke?" she stated in a very cavalier manner. "I am me and I ain't stupid to smoke in front of my children, but I don't smoke and that is the point. I'll take another drug test." Without further inquiries, the guard summoned a supervisor for assistance.

Dolly, a diminutive woman, had a rusty medium brown complexion that defied the true definition of color, and in a way, implied a need for attention to personal hygiene, bordering on being disheveled. Her color seemingly and expressively evoked an inquiry from one who has never come face to face with a female figure that pleaded for engagement in conversation.

She was part of the indigenous Taino people of Puerto Rico, appeared to be Amerindian of South America, but knew nothing about the island or anywhere else beyond what was told to her by friends and family. Dolly left Puerto Rico at age six with her birth mother and siblings to live in Florida but transitioned to New York City. The Projects became the only option, at that time, for such a family of meager means, low academic achievement, and limited options for upward mobility.

Her attire spoke of another era when the kaleidoscopes of colors were part of the decorum during the hippie culture. There seemed to be a hidden façade that was secretly tucked away far beneath her clothing and facial grins. There was a giggle of laughter, as she began running the fingers of her right hand back and forth between her left armpit. Dolly continued scratching and alternated from one armpit to the other. An inquisitive look at Dolly's indulgence triggered an outburst, "What?"

With piercing eyes directed at the author, and suggestive to the onlooker that something was out of the ordinary, Dolly continued to scratch her arms, legs, and head with the synchronization of an orchestra conductor. The scratching and movement of the body took on an intoxicating rhythm and an artistic proficiency as her fingers moved into an orifice here and there. Dolly seemed to enjoy her pastime of scratching.

She appeared to be lost in another period as she rambled to unseen entities. Dolly was less than five feet tall with a diminishing physical structure that demanded a scratch here and there, and under the arm pits, while a childlike smile engulfs a giggle of innocence. She continued her indulgence.

A female supervisor, with a wandering eye in search of the unknown, appeared in a few minutes. Without engaging Dolly, the supervisor whispered to another female worker, and looked directly at her. They immediately assumed a frown and a look of disgust and impatience.

"That one over there appears to be under the influence of something, maybe drugs, and alcohol. What a piece of work and only God can help her." uttered the supervisor. "Who are you talking about, not me I hope, what's up? I need help. Where are my children?" inquired Dolly.

Dolly began using illicit substances when her husband returned home from fighting in the Vietnam War. He felt betrayed by America- there was nothing done by the United States government for returning veterans to make life bearable. It was a period when returning veterans were looked upon as misfits and outcasts. Her deceased husband returned home to face a rejected nation.

The Vietnam War was destructive and it reaped havoc on the lives of many returning veterans who were injured, and suffered posttraumatic syndrome problems. The American people did not welcome home the fighting men as heroes, but as rejects. Jobs were limited, and the possibility of gaining employment was a remote and distant dream. Veterans of this war were cast away, and forgotten by the federal government.

The Vietnam war from 1954-1975 and the counterculture of the 1960's, all wrapped up in one, proved to be destructive in many ways and especially for Dolly, her husband, and subsequently for the children. Their lives became a battleground of survival, and by any means necessary, to carve out an existence in an environment inundated with illicit activities and engulfed with drugs of every kind. She, like other residents in the community who were subsistent and dependent on every form of entitlements, saw selling drugs and making a buck as innocuous, despite seeing the ravaging effects such activities have had on their lives.

Dolly's husband was one of the last combatants to return home late 1975, after spending two stints in Vietnam. On the night before Justin's return home, a sniper killed his best friend and comrade. Because of a bonding relationship, before and after combat, Justin accompanied the body back to his home state for burial. Justin took his friend's death personal, and thus begun his sojourn into the bowels of further addiction; he became addicted to heroin while in Vietnam.

Justin not only accompanied the deceased body back to the United States, but 20 kilos of 90% pure heroin that replaced the disemboweled intestines of his friend. Justin was thinking on becoming rich and he was in a hurry. Just becoming rich in the manner he chose would devastate his family in a hurry.

Justin had acquired an addiction to heroin while in the trenches of Vietnam. He was fighting an overseas war, which was very alien to most draftees, and now he was engaged in a personal war of addiction. It did not matter to Justin, while in Vietnam, if he survived the atrocities of the war or not; he was only living for anyway to alleviate the pain that he was experiencing and witnessing every day.

The need and availability of heroin were everywhere upon his return to the United States. All large cities at that time became a Mecca for illicit drugs. Justin had 20 kilos of quality heroin, and a dependency too. It was troubling for Justin, who suffered from the latent and lingering effects of his friend's death, and the uncertainty of his ability to cope with the world he returned to after years of fighting in a foreign country without a vision of winning. He rejected and shunned efforts to address his psychological issues and became aloof from everyone.

Justin, upon his return home, became the man, so to speak, in the projects where he peddled his poison. He had what everyone needed, quality heroin. It was the best dope available on the streets. It was his hood, as he referred to the community within that enclave that condoned illicit activities and coalesced to promote such activities. Seemingly, the gentry displayed a belief that their world functioned as it does, because it just belonged to the owners and possessors of bling, as jewelry is called by most in a certain age group. Bling suggested the attainment of success.

The man was described as free spirited, and as such, created a loyal pool of new customers simply by giving out small samples of his deadly product. He wanted to make his mark, so he built a loyal following. According to Dolly, everyone was getting nice, meaning high on drugs, as she was on a daily basis, for just being there. Everyone seemingly became lethargic and floating in an empty space of his or her own dimension.

Samples of heroin were seemingly free and gained a following because as the saying goes, there is no such thing as a free lunch. The gentry were hooked and succumbing to brand identity with loyalty. Names like killer and snow white were attached to the product to identify an allegiance and create market share for the product. The neighborhood seemed like a carnival filled with customers pacing the sidewalks in pursuit of quality product that was granted by extending credit for heroin purchases. It was a sight to behold- people looking like zombies going back and forth on the same block waiting to get credit. As was generally understood, the terms of credit were for 5 days only and with interest payments of 50% for good customers with an occupational history, and to those who paid in the established period. Business was good.

However, for those who received monthly public assistance stipends the rate became 100% interest in 30 days with a maximum credit of $150. Dolly compared the rates to that of a pawnbroker and the Native American payday loan repay, where interest rates can go as high as 300%. She described her husband as a savior to those in need of a quick fix of heroin. It was all business transactions.

Dolly indulged in eight ball samplings of heroin with her three siblings. It was the top of the line concoction. She and everyone else enjoyed a free taste of horse-street vernacular for heroin- while they were meandering throughout the environs of their public housing complex. Everyone was happy, but this was short lived.

All the free loaders, within a short period became addicted converts to heroin, and needed a daily fix. The free loaders became purchasers with meager means, and relied on credit to satisfy their addiction. Credit was extended to the date when welfare checks became payable at the local cash checking center. The transactions became revolving credit and payable in different forms and methods. Cash and money orders were preferred, but bartering of high priced merchandise, jewelry, and precious metals at rock bottom prices was the routine when customers exhausted their funds. Business was good and lively.

People converted food stamps into cash at the neighborhood delicatessens. Their survival depended on this type of activity due to high rentals in the area. It was a quick conversion that yielded a fee for deli owners and this enabled customers to continue their journey of dependency, which in a large number of cases, ultimately led to neglect of themselves, extended family members, and children. As the vicious cycle and propensity to consume were established, customers buzzed around and congregate on certain blocks in the neighborhood as bees attracted to the honeycomb.

People became addicted and used heroin everyday as their insatiable appetite for the drug grew. As the cravings for heroin grew,so did their creative methods of procuring illicit substances go beyond selling food stamps or stealing from relatives, who tried to motivate them to stop using alcohol or illicit drugs, and in particular, heroin. Most eventually stole merchandise from large stores because everything of value they had owned was gone for drugs. For a few, alternative schemes developed to satisfy their addiction.

Dolly started prostituting, and was jailed twice for solicitation, while her siblings were boosting (shoplifting) at the large department stores in shopping mall and on busy areas where tourists frequent. Trading her body created earnings to satisfy her addiction. Her apartment became a warehouse for stolen clothing, handbags, and jewelry. She considered the bartering of illegal gains a god sent to the poor, who wanted and placed a high personal value on the acquisition of things as symbols of attainment. It was business for Dolly.

Customers were only concerned with just being in possession of unknown origins of original merchandise or copies, of the original product. Dolly was simply providing needed services in a niche market. Not only were these transactions ongoing with tenants in the public housing complex, but buyers came from every neighborhood to make their purchases. On a few occasions, when the merchandise was an original, a personal delivery would be made. It was business as usual.

There was a continuous flow of people in and out of Dolly's apartment, while two nebulous and androgynously looking women stood outside the front door as lookouts for the police. Most of the stolen merchandise in the apartment was of premium quality and carefully selected during boosting-stealing- at upscale stores. Coach and Michael Kors handbags, Rolex watches, Jones shirts, and American eagle brand were immediately targeted. Orders were also placed by buyers a week in advance. It was business to everyone in the projects and it continued for a few years until successful interdiction by undercover police.

Justin who was snorting heroin when he returned home transformed himself into a junkie injecting five times a day. The last time we encountered he described his daily routine as chasing the high, and predicted his own demise. I subsequently learned that he overdosed twice and succumbed to a deadly batch of heroin.

Dolly, whom I subsequently learned was terminal, expired after long periods of hospitalizations.

Within a few moments, a familiar male face appeared from the opened elevator door. Before exiting the elevator, a hand held the opened door and while a head stuck, out and carefully glanced to the left and right, as if he were trying to avoid someone. It seemed from those repetitive actions by clients that they were always on the lookout for something or someone. Clients always seemed ambivalent, while apprehension always lingers with suspicion of intervention by personnel during office visits. Clients were always on the alert when summoned to the field office, or are required to make an appearance. Suspicions of yesteryear continued and fueled by anecdotes of personal tragedies within the agency.

It was Lewis, as I would call him, because I remember him built like Joe Lewis, the boxer. He was a client who came to the field office every week like clockwork. He appeared at the office to congregate with other clients who frequented the agency without having an appointment. A few appeared like fixtures, and always present seeking assistance or advice or a referral. Lewis exchanged pleasantries with some and others with a few handshakes and hugs and clowning around like old compatriots.

Lewis stepped off the elevator and immediately assumed his swagger as he walked over to the reception area with a big smile on his face.

"Good morning, I hope you all had a good week like mine was before coming here", was Lewis' way of announcing his presence as he cordially interacted with the security guard, who was accustomed to seeing him every week.

"How you doing, I haven't seen you in a few weeks. Everything's good, you look good, how about that?" Lewis asked in a jovial manner as if he were engaging a close friend in conversation. With a big grin on his face, Lewis moved his head from side to side, in a bobbing and weaving manner, and with precision and artistry as he strutted across the floor. He was always entertaining with his antics.

"Had a little family vacation?" asked the security guard in a cordial manner. By vacation, the guard meant Lewis' customary venture into phase one, detoxification, leading to rehabilitation. Lewis admitted that he indulged in this behavior whenever he thought that his body needed to be purified from substances. Lewis habitually returned to his old modus operandi; drinking excessive alcohol. He was no different from the others in his quest for the spirits.

"Let me touch base with my main man." Lewis stated in a demanding manner as his hands reached over the front desk.

Lewis made the usual weekly trip to the field office to get money to purchase Night Train, a favorite alcohol beverage chosen by the poor, and most often by alcoholics in the inner city neighborhoods. He would settle for nothing less than the bottom of the barrel spirits. Lewis confided in me that his addictive nature to alcohol was due to his genetic predisposition. According to Lewis, his father drank himself to death; his uncle drank first thing in the morning to start the day until his death; his sister drinks a six pack of beer daily; and all extended family members drank to inebriation. Lewis indicated that alcoholism was the family's curse, and they accepted it as such without any inquiry to validate the genetic predisposition.

Lewis accepted the status of alcoholic dependent, but always stated that cocaine "crept up" on him from small daily indulgences. Lewis admitted that he was now using eight dime ($10) bags of cocaine daily. The cost- $80- was demanding, and this was troubling for him.

Lewis informed all his caseworkers, counselors, psychiatrists, therapist, and intervention specialists over the past 20 years, that cocaine had "messed him up" and did something to his brain. Yet, he remained in recovery for twenty years. Lewis, with conviction, stated to me after a long conversation, that he needed something else to address his dependencies on cocaine and alcohol. Counseling was not doing it for him!

Lewis was still in recovery, but this was not voluntary. Lewis acquiesced to requests to enter rehabilitation to save his children from going into the foster care system a third time. He wanted to be a father to the children in the same home with his wife. He did what was ordered but felt the compulsion to use illicit substances.

Lewis gave an accounting of his journey and subsequent dependency on alcohol and crack cocaine when he resided in public housing. As many residents, trapped in the inner city public housing projects that were engulfed with ongoing drug activities, the availability was easy and effortless; drugs were issued on revolving credit just like financing of credit cards. It was simply the purchase of drugs on credit. The business of illicit drug sales was conducted like an ordinary supermarket purchase of food items. It was that simple in the projects.

Lewis had a very productive and successful career as a broker of illicit substances, but his mistake was dabbling with his products on social occasions. Over time, social indulgences became progressively daily routine. Not only was the indulgence of cocaine on a daily basis routine, but the quantity and quality of usage increased dramatically to the point where affordability became a daily taxing exercise for him.

Because he was using his own product, earnings from sales to his retail customers became miniscule. He was now spending more and using more of his own product for his personal use. On occasion, he would short weight or steal 25% of a three gram sale to satisfy his urgent need. He was simply doing what other low level dealers were doing. It was no secret to customers. Customers were not walking around with a scale to determine weight and this allowed him to pilfer easily. Apparently, size, not weight, seemed to be the criteria that determined a double sale, and Lewis knew that this required him to adulterate the product.

His insatiable appetite for cocaine subsequently caused him to be financially indebted to his supplier. He was always behind in payment and seemed to never to catch up to what he initially owed to his supplier. Interest payments were at the heart of his inability to fulfill his obligation to pay off the debt. Credit became revolving, as was his indebtedness to servitude. It became a crazy and vicious cycle.

Because of Lewis' indebtedness to his supplier, there was no option other than to acquiesce to requests by his supplier to transport illicit drugs on several occasions from the south to a few cities. Lewis stated that these demands predisposed him to possible incarceration or death for failure to comply. He was able to pay off his debts in a few trips. But the fear of being caught and jailed for a long time played a direct role in elevating his blood pressure. Medications came to his rescue to alleviate his stress.

Not only was Lewis using cocaine but also he was maintaining an intimacy with alcohol. Alcohol was nothing new to Lewis. The journey with alcohol started in his teens, as somewhat, a right that transitions the male into manhood, and with the implicit approval of the patriarch, who invoked that manhood must be displayed with the indulgence of alcohol called "dharu". He was now a man and dependent on alcohol and addicted to cocaine.

In the old country, as Lewis refers to his place of birth, there was a drink for everything, and I mean for EVERYTHING! Take a shot, was the term used to initiate the drinking of alcohol. The offering of a drink became reflexive during all interaction, whether social or not, and was ingrained in the culture, as a national past time.

In many Caribbean nations over the centuries, sugar cane was grown for export and to produce molasses, the main ingredient in the making of alcoholic spirits. It was only natural for natives, who had easy access to spirits in the rum producing regions, to be consumers of their own product, and use volumes of alcohol during any celebration. It was part of the culture.

Having a few drinks after work each day was expected by the gentry. But, a failure by a male to indulge in a few drinks after work was seen by most as less than sociable and often he would be described as soft and unable to hold his sauce, as in alcohol. This ingrained acceptance of alcohol, as a part of the social culture, was troubling because no one wanted to be ostracized for not having a drink or two after the completion of a tedious task. Just the fear of being shunned created submission to the inevitable drinks after work behavior.

It was no different for Dolly, who referred to Puerto Rico as PR, with a sense of eagerness and urgency to return to the island. Her early memories of PR seemed not to exist, yet she spoke of goings on in PR, as if she spent her adolescent days there. She knew of San Herman, Ponce, and Old San Juan, and spoke as if she knew of the native ongoing celebrations and affinity for rums. She spoke from the stories told to her by her mother and close relatives.

For Dolly and Lewis, returning to their places of birth was a remote possibility. Both were only able to identify with their place of birth and nothing more.

Lewis spontaneously reflected about times in the old country during his adolescence. He knew that the national past time, embedded in the collaboration of humans around a few drinks, was normal. However, a few drinks meant a few bottles, and was seen as the thing to do by adults. Lewis was a part of that experience, but now indulging with alcohol was no longer a passing state of celebrating an event of significance. The indulgence became the morning routine preceding breakfast.

Lewis confessed that he needed alcohol early in the morning. "It's like that in the morning" he stated, as he stared at his trembling hands while his fingers kept moving involuntarily as if he were in rhythmical and musical form. Lewis had the shakes.

"It's my quicker-picker-upper," declared Andrew, displaying a saintly air. He had 18 years of involvement with some 12 rehabilitation programs specifically designed for alcohol abuse; always perfunctory in his involvement. A few of the programs he attended were inpatient, lasting twelve to eighteen months. Upon discharge, Andrew, like all alcoholics, was instructed and required to maintain contact with clinicians, caseworkers, psychologists, counselors, and psychiatrists. Andrew was ok with such mandates.

Andrew continued his perfunctory involvement with rehabilitation and under supervision; he reported to his counselor twice each week for the duration of the mandate. But the urge to indulge was beyond his control, and he knew and understood the ramifications that any violation would immediately terminate his release. Andrew, like most clients, understood orders, and was committed to adhering to all directives, but could not stop the impulse from indulging; he tried.

Andrew attended all required sessions of rehabilitation and subsequent follows ups, and even received letters of successful completions. Two programs conferred upon him the status of exemplary with testimonials attesting to his success.

He understood how to use word association and body language, especially during a clinical intake, to create the effect that penetrates and infiltrates the psyche of the clinician to evoke empathy. Andrew knew how to use empathy to gain the favor of personnel at the many programs he was involved with over the years. He knew each program's requirements and structure. He even did his own collateral inquiries on counselors in his plot to work the system, as he described his shenanigans, with the keen sense of a researcher analyzing data.

He attended a few rehabilitation programs where sessions were held three times each week. He even refrained from using any form of alcohol twenty four hours proceeding each session, and submitted to random urine samples, as per protocol. Interestingly enough, Andrew spoke with a grin on his face, claimed that he always needed a few drinks after each contact session with their counselor. The propensity to drink consciously, as is done by alcoholics like Andrew and others, can be attributed to the direct result from permanent changes in the body that requires and demands alcohol for functionality.

Alcoholics submitting to urine analysis only, and as the yardstick of a substance free status, give them freedom to cheat while remaining in compliance. It was simply too easy to cheat in order to remain in compliance with either the Department of Motor Vehicles, or any contracted agency in charge of monitoring and randomly testing a client. They were smart. The games continued. The manipulations became routine to remain ahead of whatever was deemed as mandated.

Another client, whom I shall call Hun because he fits the profile associated with Attila the Hun- he was brutal to the bottle and his self. If you recall, the Huns, a nomadic Mongolian people who invaded Europe in the 4th and 5th centuries, were brutal warriors.

Hun led drinking sessions by establishing his prowess at what he termed as out drinking others. At times, Hun continued drinking while his associates were completely inebriated to the point of stupor. Hun boasted of his abilities at consuming alcohol, as if this ability transcended him to another plateau that was unreachable by anyone else. Drinking marathons elevated him to a new status, with a coronation for his competitive achievement. He was king at drinking!

Hun's favorite was brown rum, which he described as, superior in quality. He was proud of his choice of spirits because it gave him identity with his place of birth and nothing more. Hun remained a warrior at the bottle and paid his price.

Hun had been drinking since his early adulthood, and over the years built a reputation as someone who can, hold his liquor, as the saying goes. He was known as the one to trust behind the wheel after an evening of socializing. Drinking associates described him, despite his constant state of intoxication, as the designated driver, who knew his way home by heart. It seemed simply insane to trust someone who was completely drunk behind the wheel of an automobile filled with people; yet he was complimented by those of his crowd.

Ladies often described Hun as an excellent driver after he consumed a quart of rum. He was consuming for over twenty five years and remained accident free until recently. He was embarrassed being in such a position after failing a sobriety tests, and then incarcerated for twenty-four hours. This never happened to him. But was it a wakeup call? Problematic for him was his employment in an industry that was unfavorable to drunks and addicts. His job was secure up to that point, but a conviction for alcohol presented disaster that would have an impact on his pension, which was five years hence. Complicated because he was warned of his drinking during lunch breaks; detailed the consequences of any alcohol conviction, and counseled to seek professional intervention to avoid the disaster that fell upon him.

Hun was described by an associate as being on "remote control" after consuming a few bottles of rum during any drinking session with the same crowd of colleagues. This associate spoke of Hun in a mystical manner, as if Hun had powers specifically bestowed upon him by the supernatural being, which allowed him to navigate his way home accident free. Hun was a champion drinker.

Hun, while in the privacy of his home, enjoyed a combination of rum mixed with beer; the latter was described as the chaser to dilute the mixture. Brand loyalty to any manufacturer had no significance for Hun. However, this combination, according to him, was a special deal, when something significant took place that affected the family positively. Hun was always in a celebratory mood.

Indeed, there was an unknown and mystical quality, coupled with ritual, that followed Hun's filling his glass, and with a celebratory action, exclaimed, "I'll drank to that!". This exclamation was always followed the cultural ritual of recognition of the elders of a bygone era. It was a farewell gesture and reminder of leaving the homeland of Africa for the unknown qualities of the New World.

Hun, like most people of African ancestry, gave praises to the ancestors by throwing a small amount of spirits into any corner, in whatever room drinking was taking place. Jah Rastafari! The latter intonation gave a distinct flare of satisfaction to the indulgence.

Hun described his drinking sessions as a meeting of the minds on a daily basis. Hun compared his daily association for a drinking session as similar to Plato's symposium but not on the subject of homosexual love as the dialogue addresses. Men, according to Hun, are expected to clear their minds in the afternoon and indulge in political jesting, while alcohol titillates the imagination.

Hun attended alcohol rehabilitation sessions twice per week, for one year at one of the many programs in the cities he lived. Participants cavalierly stated that he or she was in a program. Programs were everywhere. But what needs were they fulfilling? More importantly, was their presence beyond being there to score attendance, and indulge in superficial and "cosmetic psychotherapeutic intervention", as have been described by some professionals, to establish stability? Many were just attending by mandates of the courts.

Programs, although mandated and has an organizational flow chart of responsibilities, and in many cases adequate staff, are maintained as a revolving door for alcoholics and drug addicts. It appears that the ardent efforts by clinicians are focused for changes in their clients, and as such, inadvertently gives free rein for clients to violate mandates set by judicial authority. Many abusers remained the same old heads from previous programs that they attended. Many clients claimed that their relationship building with clinicians was not lasting or bonding, because clinicians, as they claimed, were shuffled from one program to another while assuming titles of little significance. Clients, who were acclimated to the workings of programs, expressed their frustrations at having to restate their issues or history to constantly changing staff with newly assigned titles. Everyone had a title to define him or herself.

Such programs were mills where attendance was mandated and participation only perfunctory. Mills are nothing more than revolving doors for the acclimated and self- endorsed alcoholics and drug addicts.

Hun attended mandatory DMV (Department of Motor Vehicles) classes every Saturday. As far as Hun was concerned, DMV classes were nothing more than a joke, filled with repetitious and boring information, and lacking in appeal. Hun's only focus, while attending DMV sessions, was the ending time and nothing more. He needed a drink after each session.

Hun's attendance at alcohol rehabilitation was perfect. His weekly urine testing samples failed to detect alcohol. Hun was only required to submit urine samples and nothing more. This requirement was a gift to him, and permission to continue in his indulgence. Hun was drank the same amount and complied with all court orders. He understood the diffusion of alcohol, and drank during periods of non- contact with his counselor.

Hun was a success on paper. He succeeded in succumbing to alcohol poisoning when he crashed his minivan into a pole.

However, success, although defined and accepted as coming about through incremental changes, was becoming more difficult with the passage of time for most abusers. Success and change seemed to be trapped in a revolving door of interventions, which in many cases trapped the client into a zone of never ending involvement with programs. Clients were going around in circles and with enablers in the helping professions navigating the way.

Something about the approaches to sobriety was not making sense, and I needed to find out. And finding out, demanded an immersion, through observation, into the activities of this population.

Andrew and I became respectful of each other over the years until his demise. What flowed from Andrew's conversations begged the question of validity of rehabilitation programs, beyond support for functional addicts and alcoholics. There had to be alternatives, but certainly not using the modalities we have become accustomed to in traditional programs. Troubling was the expenditure appropriated by Federal, State, and City mandates for rehabilitation programs and enforced by the courts.

Andrew spoke of his training in nursing and his relationship to each patient that he monitored while working at a Trauma Center. Andrew, a registered nurse, worked in emergency rooms for 15 years. During that time, he recognized his predisposition to alcohol abuse, but voluntarily drank to enhance the brain's reward centers. Andrew enjoyed the feeling, not of intoxication, but of pleasure.

A report made to the Central Registry during a hot summer day, disrupted Andrew's life, financially, professionally, and socially. He was named as abusing alcohol; using cocaine; inappropriate parenting; endangering and neglecting his six children. These allegations terrified Andrew and his future with the children.

Andrew was the caregiver for his six children whose birth mother was found to be psychiatrically incompetent. Andrew had to answer the charges. The implications for the children were devastating. The children were assigned, as a standard procedure, when a report is filed with the Central Registry, case numbers. Biographic data on each child was recorded. Physical and medical evaluations were done on each child. The children became part of the social services system.

This inking of identification of alleged abuse or neglect by the State Central Registry, immediately and permanently becomes part of an extended network of agencies within the social welfare system. Privacy was lost. Even if the allegations were determined to be unsubstantiated or unfounded, the indelible stain had been made. Source of the allegations remained anonymous. He had no defense. Children services were in total control.

In the interim, because children were involved, educational officials became involved, as well as, medical personnel who evaluated the children for abuse and neglect. To support and associate the concept of birds of a feather, all household members, despite not being named in the report of alleged drug and alcohol abuse, founded themselves, as Lewis called it, in a Dutch handcuff- a phrase commonly used throughout the Indies where individual rights become subservient to state regulations. Irreparable damage was inflicted, by an anonymous source, upon persons whose lives had been private up to that time.

A cousin, who spent intermittent periods in Andrew's household, refused to be tested and refrained from divulging any personal information to agency personnel. Everyone was angry and felt helpless because the source remained anonymous. The agency was now in everyone's business due to association and implicitly the guilty blanket covered whoever was residing in the household. Everyone was under investigation.

This type of intrusion, which has rippling effects beyond the investigation was nothing new in the lives of the indigent, the working poor, and the less informed. Because of these social conditions, two ingredients remain constant in their lives: the government bureaucratic agencies, and primarily the local police. The whole family was now involved.

Lewis and Andrew found themselves submitting to alcohol and drug screenings. They knew that testing would be positive for cocaine, marijuana, and alcohol. They also knew the periods for the diffusion of alcohol and cocaine from their systems 3-5 days, but marijuana was another issue.

Lewis and Andrew plotted to evade positive results. A call and a visit to Brandy's Health store, for its quality product line, was a mandatory in this type of situation. Brandy's Health had the solution to address all urgent needs. A decision was made to act immediately.

A call was made to Brandy's Health, a health food store. Indeed, Brandy's Health was a health food store with a major specialization and thrust. The store had a loyal customer base because of its history of concocting evasive methods and had ongoing efforts that specialized in numerous oral cocktails to mask varying drug tests, and in particular, for urine analysis. Brandy's Health had the cocktails that everyone needed whenever there was an ongoing investigation by any agency. Any one of the numerous cocktails, when ingested, masks or taints the results to read false negative or false positive or simply negative for all illicit substances. It was Brandy's business to provide favorable results, and to make sure that the customer returns for another portion.

Prices for a portion depended on the results wanted, or on the industry that would interpret the results. If you are limited on cash, the choice becomes a false negative or false positive result. Either one of the latter results would cause abusers to be retested later so that the results would read negative. This approach gives the client the additional waiting time to be tested and for diffusion of the substance. On the other hand, portions that are more expensive would guarantee a negative reading immediately.

Periods were very important for abusers who were having a urine analysis. The client who smoked marijuana stalls the testing for 30 days to ensure that all THC is out of the system. On the other hand, the alcoholic and drug addict has the upper hand by stalling the test for 4 days. All drug screening results, using urine, will read in the negative ranges once the client adheres to the ranges. Follicle testing, which was costly and detected the presence of illicit substances in the system for one year, was only requested for clients who were continuously problematic. Since finances were scarce, urine testing became the more affordable method.

Compounding the problems, timely notification of drug screening results; neither abuser nor worker would get the results for days or weeks or more, the agency remained in limbo, unable to make a determination, which would enable workers to intervene judiciously for a finding of abuse or neglect. It became hit or miss, and a waste of resources trying to determine if a client was indulging. Nevertheless, measures were in place to evaluate and determine the appropriate course of action, to ensure the safety and the wellbeing of the population under its mandate.

A gap in communication with screening centers and a failure of personnel to maximize their use of technology to gain efficiency were dominant themes throughout the agency. There was no urgency in an agency inundated with meetings and conferences to reiterate the known. There were always training sessions that were void of education or celebrations of inconsequential issue or memorandums lacking substance, and meetings on procedures to fulfill mandates. This time gap provided abusers many opportunities to obfuscate a second test by disingenuous methods, such as, claiming to be ill and on medications. It became a cat and mouse game.

Stalling remained only one evasive tool in the box of tricks used by abusers who knew that a urine sample would prove to be positive for illicit drugs or alcohol. Unorthodox methods to mask urine samples were also used by a few. The ingenuous nature of abusers in using nature's own to mask drug screening results was simply stunning, yet creative. Never take the client for granted or lacking the ability to make choices, whether good or bad. Clients are, as the saying goes, only human and capable of making realistic choices to preserve their integrity.

On one occasion, while accompanying a male abuser to a testing center to submit urine samples, his wandering eyes were obvious to any onlooker that something was about to happen. His eyes became selective for dog excrement. It just boggles the imagination to think that dog excrement was important, especially when living in New York City, and plays a role in the world lived by the alcoholic and drug addict.

Feces, as a survival tool, have contaminating and masking properties specifically suited to make urine samples useless. Using this approach simply extends the new testing for a later time and allows the client to prepare himself for another test that will result in a negative reading for all illicit substances and alcohol. By taking such a measure the client is able to move beyond testing, remain relevant and to have access to whatever the system, as most people refer to entitlements, stipulated as the minimum degree of care to be provided to children in their care.

As we walked over to the testing center, I kept my eyes on every motion as he meandered on his way to be tested. At times, he would stop abruptly to visually determine which piece of excrement he would select. It was if he had a special selection skill in deception. He scanned the area as if he was a robot programed for a specific task, and in this case, it was simply feces collection.

When the choice was made, he quickly stuck his index finger into a chosen lump and carefully wrapped the finger with a napkin, and spontaneously grunted an outburst of joy and satisfaction. I was dumfounded at this spectacle. He was happy with his find. I was disgusted at the sight. Here I was on the sidewalk and accompanying a cesspool to the testing center.

"Oh Jesus, he smells terrible, let him in first!" was the greeting by the clerk in the reception area, as she hurriedly motioned him to a cubicle to urinate. The clerk hastily instructed him that upon completion to present his cup of urine to the handling clerk for analysis. The latter method of handling the urine was known as the unbroken chain-hand of exchange of urine being applied here.

"We get all kinds and all day long, our clients are real diverse, Jesus!" stated the clerk, as she looked directly at me. I can't believe the things some of them would do." She handed him a cup to urinate into for his sample. I shrugged my shoulders while motioning my hands to infer silent concurrence with her statement.

He was in and out of the facility in fifteen minutes. He had an expression of accomplishment on his face as he took a breath of relief. Despite stating earlier that he was in a hurry to take care of urgent business, John made his requests.

"Don't forget my tokens, and I mean round trip" was his initial request. ACS granted funds to clients to go back and forth from visitations and testing centers. He lived in walking distance of the office, but far enough and beyond the catchment area, to qualify for the reimbursement of $4.00.

"Do you have any leftover food that I can have?" he asked, as he scratched his forehead in a manner to suggest that that more demands were about to be made. "The children beds are broken. You should come over and look. They can use new beds. The summer is coming and they do not have appropriate clothing yet, and funds are tight." He continued. "Got a question for you, but not sure if you would answer." I stated. "Try me.", he responded with a wide smile on his face. He was now tolerable to be in close proximity of after using the bathroom. Soap did little to mask the odor of feces. John was putrid and smelt more like rancid oil with an annoying pungency that permeated the environment. John's presence was announced by odor and needed no introduction because he was known by agency staff.

"What's up with the dog shit?" I inquired. "What are you talking about?" he asked with a strange and puzzling look on his face. He looked directly at me, while he reflexively kept looking over his shoulders in a scanning manner that became mechanical and suspicious. He started to fidget. "You know what I am talking about, be straight with me." I stated. He moved closer to me and whispered, "It's the old game when you're broke, man. A little dog shit does it every time. Come on brother, you know the hood, you got to be in the know." He stated with an air of expertise granted to those in the ghetto, and to those aware with things needed to either survive the daily intrusions by officials to arrest or remove for future imprisonment.

"You know how it is. The hood is an education. You got to f—k it man! He stated with trepidation, and gesticulated with flailing arms outreached to the heavens. "Is this an interrogation or what?" he asked. He seemed aggravated by the question for some unknown reason. "Man you know the deal. Too many programs over the years, and they are the same. I've listened to all those clowns from Washton, and you know that's top of the line next to Betty Ford, and Smithers and, I don't mean any disrespect." He revealed.

"Recovery and all that shit. Man gives me a break. They really believe you cannot think. What's up! What's up?" he shouted. He continued rambling incoherently, as he paced the floor back and forth. He was in another world and oblivious to everything. At times, he would abruptly stop. His eyes had a piercing effect attached to a stare far away. No words were uttered.

As he kept his distance, he swiftly breezed by my side. I was invisible to his presence. He seemed to have been mentally transported somewhere else and in time. He was only physically present. Occasionally, while mumbling, he would stop abruptly to stare at the ceiling and burst out laughing for no apparent reason. It sounded as if he was creating the mimicking sound of a monkey in front of a demanding audience. After venting for what seemed like eternity, he dropped himself into a chair and asked for some water. He was exhausted and out of breath. He gulped down the glass of water with urgency.

Referring to Washton Institute, Betty Ford Clinic, and Smithers Drug Rehabilitation Center spoke of reputation and success. All three rehabilitation centers tailored their programs to the client's specific needs. Washton treated those addicted to cocaine, while Betty Ford's specialty design was directed at alcohol abusing clients. Smithers came with money and social standing to gain acceptance. According to literature from these programs the one fit all approach to the healing process for those afflicted with the stressful effects of dependency and addiction, is not used. These programs were tailored made for those with the financial means.

Daryl Strawberry and Dwight Gooden, two great athletes, inducted into the Mets Hall of Fame in 2010, were in rehabilitation numerous times at one or more of the centers mentioned. The former athletes entered rehabilitation for cocaine and the latter for alcohol abuse.

Since entering rehabilitation and subsequently relapsing, Gooden and Strawberry have built into their lexicon, words such as, in recovery and recovering, as symbols of just being human with faults. These phrases were taught and learned by participants in rehabilitation, and are used by them to describe who they have become.

Strawberry has now recognized that there is no known effective prescription medication available for treating cocaine addiction beyond a good support system and being in a new environment. Gooden, on the other hand, has recognized his being as alcoholic, and has chosen a different way to manage his life for his own survival. Darryl Strawberry and Dwight Gooden have chosen divergent paths.

Dwight, tired of rehabilitation, chose prison as a shield from the demons and for his alcohol withdrawal. Darryl, on the other hand, chose the therapeutic approach, and committed himself to effect change in the lives of others. The Darryl Strawberry Residential Treatment Program in St. Cloud, Florida, opened in 2014, attested to his commitment for a drug free existence.

I was assigned a case where alcohol and cocaine were allegedly being used by the step father of two teenage girls who were under his supervision a number of times. At his trial in family court, he admitted to using cocaine, not alcohol, and inadequate guardianship of the children. He was ordered by the Court to attend alcohol/ drug rehabilitation and parenting classes. It was further stipulated by family court that the step father should not be assigned the responsibilities for the care and supervision of either child. Other stipulations were in the Order, directed at the birth mother, to ensure the safety of all parties concerned.

As the assigned caseworker, it became incumbent upon me to make referrals to several programs seeking acceptance for the perpetrator, birth mother, and the children. I adhered to the Orders and made contacts with numerous programs that provided the needed services within the catchment area.

The step father whom called Trini immigrated to the United States from the Caribbean during the heights of tensions in the 1990s. He graduated from an Ivy League school, with a degree in electrical engineering, and had a professional license. He was then employed by a large multinational corporation in the aerospace industry. Trini was salaried at $120,000 annually.

After speaking to intake personnel at several programs, where openings for new client were available, I immediately contacted Trini by telephone to provide the referral, and for him to select the program that meets his needs. I also sent written information to him about each program to the address he provided at that time.

"Trini, I have good news for you regarding a few programs" I began the conversation on the phone. "Which ones, and where are they located?" he asked.

I read out all the names of programs in his catchment area, and advised that slots were available for immediate registration.

There was total silence on the telephone. I could hear in the background, noises and sounds like a train going through a tunnel and blowing, hissing wind. It was a long wait before a voice responded.

"Are you still there?" I inquired. "Yea I'm here, but those programs you mentioned, I hate to say, are for runts. You know what I mean?" Trini stated with an apprehensive tone. "What do you mean? Help me out, explain." I inquired. "Well, it's the caliber of the participants in the program. I've been told by my assistant who's here that those programs are only for junkies and misfits." Trini stated sarcastically, with overtones of condescension.

"Those programs that I mentioned are for persons who are not only addicted to cocaine, alcohol, licit and illicit substances; but for those seeking to free themselves from addiction and dependency." I interjected. "I need to be in a program with people of similar educational and social backgrounds. How am I going to relate to junkies and cognitively impaired people like those? I am no junkie or misfit." Trini commented.

"Then what do you suggest I do to assist you so that you can comply with the Court's orders?" I asked. "I need a program with class and where the big boys go." was Trini's response. "I can explore both programs, but they are quite costly." I advised Trini. "Who cares about the cost, just get me into something with class. I just can't handle those sorry ass sons of bitches who want to make me look like a bad person." Trini rambled.

Two days later Trini learned of his acceptance into the program of his choice. It was at a very expensive and upscale program that met his desire. He was happy and requested the contact date.

The city and location filled the needs of Trini. The program gave him the flexibility to attend rehabilitation sessions in a secure and private environment while maintaining full time employment. He attended all sessions and completed all requirements. Documentation was received verifying Trini's compliance.

A month later while I was in attending a conference in another city, a distinctive voice greeted me in the most unusual manner, as if prior association was established over the years. The voice had a resonance of a sing along melody that suggested a native of Trinidad & Tobago.

"How are you doing?" inquired the voice.

The brain was at work cashing the memory to connect the voice to a name, or a country, or even a continent. The accent sounded one way that led to a mistaken geographical location, but the octave was similar to fool the unfamiliar ears. It was Trini, whose early years on the twin islands of Trinidad & Tobago accounted for the accent. He was a transplant from another region of the globe. He, like a few who were globally conscious, connected me to Carrega Ligure, a town in the Piedmont region of Italy, and the Sicilian influences and the connection to my paternal great grand ancestors from Madera, an island off the Portuguese coast.

Trini was giving a lecture on leadership qualities and was looking for additional reading material on the subject. Out of Control by Zbigniew Brzezinski and Peter Drucker's Post-Capitalist Society were necessary to compliment Thomas Sowell's Applied Economics, came to mind immediately.

"Glad to see you" I responded. "How are things going?" "Good, heading for a new assignment in a few weeks before going overseas on a busy five-year contract. There has to be something else than is dispensed in programs. It has to assist one to advance towards a substance free existence. I completed all phases during my eighteen months of rehabilitation, yet it seemed that there was a missing piece to addiction that was not known," stated Trini. "I am also trying to understand the something else, beyond the psychological." I responded, while pondering Trini's statement on addiction.

"I tell you, there is something that is not addressed by clinicians at rehab. There has to be something going on internally and I mean physically, not psychologically, that can be promulgated for the betterment of those who just cannot stop drinking or drugging all the time". "We will continue seeking for the answer to that inquiry", was the response to that troubling thought.

"Tired of all this shit, it is getting to me. Man have I tried, but something brings me back to the bottle!" stated one of my clients during an intake session, as if he wanted to try something else besides being on the continuum of programs. "I can't stop drinking. The programs help to keep me focused, but they are all the same, wanting to know my family history. I've talked to all of them about that, don't they read prior evaluations?" he questioned himself. "That quickie detox, I've had it! It is like cleaning a suit. You wear it and it gets dirty. So, you clean it again, and the process continues." he continued.

He described himself as regular detox person, as others did, from their continuous and habitual detoxifications. He went into detoxification programs at all municipal hospitals numerous times. As usual, before admission, he would have all his medical requirements- TB and physical tests- completed 24 hours before, at one of the many medical facilities he frequently visited. He cared less about costs and believed that services were provided by the federal government for everyone to use as needed.

John entered rehabilitation whenever he needed a break from using excessive alcohol. At times, he described going into detox as the mini vacation for him to think. He spoke of detoxification as if it were a rite of passage.

"In confidence, don't write this down. I got your word?" John inquired. "Try me". I responded. "You know, you and a few of the brothers working here know the deal." John muttered.

"What do you mean by the deal?" I inquired. "We live in the hood, you know what I'm talking about, and you feel me? That dog shit will do what it does to all piss. It contaminates it for real. Man, you college boys do not know a dam thing. You will know in a few days. Remember, I start the new program on Wednesday evening at 6:30pm, so don't visit then, aigh't?"

Lewis and Andrews' salvation rested upon Brandy's Health concoctions as others did, from their continuous and habitual detoxifications. These concoctions resulted from years of trial and error, mixing herbs, some of unknown origins that subsequently progressed into the fine art of herbal pharmacology.

According to local legend, Brandy's Health was the brain child of a local resident Rastafarian priest, whose members use marijuana for ceremonial purposes. This behavior and indulgence, by those Rastafarians in the community, was common knowledge to the local residents who were not troubled by the sects' indulgences.

It was reported that tensions in the community boiled over a few decades ago because of the sect doings, whatever that is supposed to mean, attire and appearances, and speech patterns that categorized them as dangerous people. The tensions resulted from the differing acceptance of marijuana use by community residents, who saw the Rastafarians as different, but not problematic, while the local authorities saw them as misfits who were intoxicated with high levels of THC, and stoned- hallucinating- at all times. To compound this perception, trying to get a working knowledge of the sect and a philosophical understanding seemed impossible. Because members spoke patois, Jamaican dialectic, and had linguistic differences, they were unable to bring to light their beliefs or contextualize the genesis of their beliefs for a discussion. Most people kept their distant because of fear of the unknown, while the police, who already saw them as misfits, kept them under scrutiny at all times.

Years ago, members who were seen smoking marijuana on their stoop received citations for violating the Federal laws. Their indulgence was nothing new, and became accepted over the years by residents as a religious ritual. Nevertheless, members arrested, fined, and placed on probation for as long as 5 years.

An independent study found that these actions by the local police came about because of so-called ignorance of the informal structure within the community coupled with federal enforcement of narcotic laws. Everyone in the community knew what was going on was illegal, and a violation of law, but did not associate the Rastafarians herbal use as dangerous or influencing the behavior of children in the community. Residents who smoked marijuana got their supplies directly from the Rastafarians.

It was difficult to understand the intrusion by authorities who lacked an understanding of the internal workings of a community, the culture, or rituals, and armed with a paucity of knowledge engulfed with contradictory information provided by sources who had inconclusive information on marijuana. It was ignorance of the unknown wrapped up in fear of the Rastafarians. Their incantations were dominant within the African diaspora, and understood in the community, but were troubling to outliers. They were smoking marijuana for decades, without incident, and known to the local precincts, yet agents were not familiar, and claimed ignorance with the sect and their sacrament. Local officials also should have known, from community policing, that was introduced by Lee

Brown, that a true Rasta, as they call themselves, would avoid and refrain from alcohol, tobacco, salt, and meats, while subscribing to a vegan diet.

Brandy's Health Care over the years, grew, and provided a needed package of services, not only to those seeking a way to pass a drug-screening test but alternative herbal medicines. Skills were developed from trial and error approaches with brewing techniques. Brandy's Health master brewer refined his techniques to the point where he became a local folk hero to confront, according to a local resident, the man, who had no understanding of the herb business. When referring to the man residents were talking about the local constabulary of the DEA (Drug Enforcement Administration) agents.

Brandy's Health now boasted their competence at portions by having a licensed pharmacist present during the working week.

At Brandy's Health, plaques of certificates attesting to affiliations and credentials adorned the walls, giving authenticity to independent research done in conjunction with other experts in alternative medicines. It was nothing more than testimonials of knowledge on display, to address the needs of the varying clients and to give assurances that each client was in the right place to get information. Patrons felt empowered by the presence of certified pseudo endorsements.

Brandy's Health provided an abundance of literature written by known nutritionists, and centrally displayed to gain mental authenticity from buyers of flushing portions. On sale, was Gary Null's book called Success to Longer Living. This book was prominently displayed to compliment Back to Eden, a classic, by Jethro Kloss. Both classics were favorites, and were bought by new patrons who were unfamiliar with the workings of their own bodies. Just for those who were interested and seeking alternative cooking, The Ayurveda Cookbook by Amadea Morningstar and Urmila Desai, which took center stage, was always recommended.

On the wall behind the counter was an enlarged photocopy of the Federal laws for the control of drugs.

The document began with The First Federal legislation - the Harrison Act of 1914- to regulate and control the production, importation, sale, purchase, or free distribution of opium, or drugs derived from opium.

Second, The Narcotic Drugs Import and Export Act of 1922, was legislation intended to eliminate the use of narcotics in this country, except for legitimate purposes.

Third, came the Marijuana Tax Act of 1937, which provides controls over marijuana, and similar to the Harrison Act.

Fourth, the Opium Poppy Control Act of 1942 that prohibits the growing of opium poppies in the United States, except under license.

Fifth, the Boggs Act of 1952 that establishes mandatory, severe penalties for conviction on narcotics charges.

Sixth, the Narcotics Control Act of 1956 was specific and directed severe penalties for those convicted of marijuana charges, and the Drug Abuse Control Amendments of 1965 with provisions to add new substances, as the need arises.

In April of 1968, the Bureau of Narcotics and the Bureau of Drug Abuse Control morphed into the Bureau of Narcotics and Dangerous Drugs to enforce Federal laws.

Interesting enough, there was recognition in 1937 that marijuana was an issue. However, it was not until 1956 that severe penalties were imposed for possession and use of marijuana throughout the United States, and possession became a federal offense. Despite focusing on just the possession of marijuana as a singular drug, The Rockefeller Drug Laws, signed on May 8, 1973, solidified this law for possession of all illicit drugs including LSD, cocaine, and heroin. In other words, all drug possession, regardless of danger levels or quantity, carried the same penalties of incarceration. Equality of sentence was of paramount importance, because of the epidemic proportions of addiction at that time. Drugs were drugs and that was all there was to it.

The Rockefeller law further exasperated the choice for advancement of the young who were first time offenders facing mandatory sentencing. Young persons, who might have been experimenting with marijuana for the first time and got caught and convicted for possession, were sentenced to as much as 15 years in jail. Characters were damaged, and upward mobility for the poor remained an illusion.

Brandy's Health was no ordinary health food store, but an environment, which provided comfort to those seeking evasive methods for drug screening. In addition, an establishment satisfied a need. In a way, the business preyed on those whose jobs were in jeopardy. Most customers were buying everything that was recommended but unnecessary, and seen by Brandy's Health sales persons as complimentary, and to ensure that everything toxin was diffused from the body. The objective was to be tested negative for all illicit substances. Patrons were buying portions of everything to be prepared when testing day arrived. "You buy additional portions just in case" was the recommendation of the sales clerk. Brandy's Health was indeed the place to get what was needed for drug screenings.

The kaleidoscope of mingling gentry at Brandy's Health suggested activities of an unknown nature. Outside the store, and in plain view of police officers, were a few double parked cars with out-of-state license plates and engines running. A few drivers, seated behind their steering wheel, appeared nervous, incongruous, and dissimilar with the racial composition of the community. As usual, police officers walked the beat, but in another direction.

Some of the patrons had a rather jejune look bordering a trance like state of nervousness. People were exiting hurriedly with small brown bags in either hand. Brandy's was at the right place and at the right time. Business transactions were ongoing and brisk.

The store was well known and operated lively with clientele of all backgrounds, races, and economic abilities. The patrons, many of them city workers, and like all other clients, demanded the best and latest formula at hand. The store was filled with patrons who were busy as bees working on a hive looking at new formulas and apparatus. Synthetic urine was available, and all products from American Screening Corporation were displayed in a special section.

In this section was The Whizzinator, one of the newest and most demanded products for drug screening. Unlike a quick flush, which is a mixture of herbs, designed to flush the kidney and liver of toxic substances so that testing would produce an acceptable and tolerable range for THC in marijuana, the Whizzinator was dried urine packed in such a way that when soaked with contaminated urine, it yields a substance free sample. The kit was available, but cost $35. A Quick Flush, similar to the Whizzinator, on the other hand, was cheaper and within the range for Lewis and Andrew.

Andrew and Lewis always kept their respective appointments for drug screening. Results always came back the same-negative-and within the acceptable range. In other words, levels of THC were present but within an acceptable range to infer proximity of location or being in the same environment with individuals who were smoking marijuana.

Before being accompanied to the testing center, Andrew and Lewis requested their return fares reimbursement of $4.00. This stipend was provided to all clients, as reimbursement for using public transportation, and who were requested to appear for either testing or for a family conference, and resided beyond the catchment area. However, some clients with several children understood this reimbursement as another source of income, when their school-aged children, who were required to pay public transportation, accompanied them to the field office. Many clients did not take public transportation to the field office; they were either transported free of charge by a friend or drove themselves. With four school aged children accompanying a parent to the field office, the windfall becomes a meager $20.

Whenever Lewis appeared at the field office accompanied by his six children, three of whom were school aged and required to pay for public transportation, the game was on the agency. Lewis went further. In addition to collecting the transportation fare stipend for him and his three schools aged children, he squeezed the system once more. Lewis chose to visit when pantry food was not available for the children at lunch time, but the children had to be fed. Another stipend, from petty cash, and worth twelve dollars was provided to feed the children. No accounting was required when a stipend was granted for children's lunch.

He did not stop at the $28.00 provided. He requested assistance with food and clothing for the children, who were inappropriately dressed for the visit and weather conditions. An assessment of the children, who appeared physically healthy, told an inferring story that things were not well in the home.

When Lewis was questioned on issues relating to the family and the children in particular, he alleged that his allocated food stamps were stolen from his mail box. He was out of food stamps and cash benefits. The agency, in order to prevent a removal and placement of the children into foster care, provided a daily stipend per child until there was a reissue of benefits. Playing the system was now in full motion. Lewis got cash, clothing, and food.

Visits of this kind were nothing new, but the methodology to gain empathy, and by extension services of every kind, took different and complex approaches in manipulation techniques. Clients appeared at the office daily to present complex and disjointed explanations for requesting assistance and to gain the attention and empathy of personnel. On a numbers of occasions, the same client would inform personnel that their birth mother died twice, in two different States in America, which resulted in family problems, and always financial.

During a face to face with Andrew at a social services office, the author overheard a conversation engulfed with methods of manipulative techniques to gain adequate housing.

Six female clients conferenced and plotted, while building consensus to implement a sound and fool proof plan. They planned to use the resources at their disposal to gain the upper hand on clinicians, and by extension, making full use of everything the system offered. They planned using intervention services as the mechanism to advocate for their immediate needs and wants. It was more WANTS than needs.

At this office, social workers and caseworkers would refer clients for rehabilitative services; accompany clients to drug screening sights; interview children and family members; and supervise visitations between siblings and parents. These services were all mandated by court orders to avoid placing children into the foster care system, while keeping the children connected to their community.

Clients knew that the focus of social services was to ensure that children are in a safe and nurturing environment, where the minimum degree of care is provided. That meant that food, clothing, shelter, medical, and social needs were adequately met by the caregiver. On many cases, there was a need for intervention services to add stability to the family's functioning. Federal, City, and State authorities contracted to agencies and under the supervision Counseling and housing for clients.

Upon inquiry, it was discovered all of these women were substance abusers with long established histories of involvement with numerous programs. Some participated at in-patient drug programs, alcohol rehabilitation, methadone maintenance, psychotherapy, and domestic violence counseling. Domestic violence was the dominant factor that seemed to play the major part in their entire decision making and it became the theme that these women used in seeking access to vital services and by extension, help for their children. Housing topped the list of needs for these women. Most agencies, which have a long history of providing good and meaningful advocacy, became the conduits the women explored for their housing needs.

To gain some perspective, think about this for a moment. A single young woman, age 20, with five children, ranging from 4 months to 5 years old, in need of adequate housing. She is estranged from all family members for years. Her parental rights were terminated. She was in foster care at age 7. A difficult history wrapped up in a vicious cycle of recidivism.

The three fathers of the five children were not involved in the children's lives. No financial support was provided by fathers, nor did the twenty year old mother of the five children wants to seek financial support through the court. This mother had no alternatives to ensure that the children were adequately cared for throughout their lives. There were no alternatives, except for them to become part of the child welfare system.

I recall a telephone report filed by an anonymous source, who resided in the same public housing facility, but a different apartment, as the family that was being reported. The source indicated that the birth mother of five children was only 20 years old and seemed overwhelmed; needed help in every aspect; children were, at times, left in the care of the mother's new boyfriend who was a teenager.

After completing all the necessary and required protocol that preceded an investigation, I headed for the projects- a cluster of public housing buildings. Because of the tainted and associated history of the entire neighborhood, workers were always advised not to conduct any investigation alone and must be accompanied by a co-worker, or better yet, seek the intervention of the local police.

I chose to be accompanied by an associate, with whom bonds were cemented during training at the Academy. We have remained friends throughout the years.

I should note that public housing, over the years, had built a reputation as an environment where life was a daily chance at survival. A chance that a resident could leave his or her apartment and be greeted by gun shots or assaulted by the nefarious characters, who lingered throughout the day in the hall ways of each floor, and in rotation, as if they were employed by the housing authority.

Just observing these characters pacing the floors as if they were in the military, suggested something less than legal, nefarious and suspicious. These young men were all armed and keeping a watchful eye, analyzing each person who entered and left the buildings. This was work of a different nature, which needed such skills. In those buildings, everyone knew what was going on but fear restricted and paralyzed residents to the extent that they implicitly condoned what they saw daily, yet silently expressed trepidation at having to succumb to such living standards.

These lookouts were there to determine, and to conclude the presence of undercover police or detectives. In public housing, crime is tackled by means of two intervening agencies- Housing and City Police- and these forces, in conjunction with undercover operatives, became the muscle to ensure safety in the buildings within the geographic cluster of the projects.

In addition to being on the alert for the police, the lookouts were directing customers, who made small daily purchases of cocaine, marijuana, and heroin, to the locations where sellers congregated for that day. Locations for the purchase of drug paraphernalia, within the complex, changed daily to avoid detection and arrests. At times, locations were random and changing each hour, while the faces of the lookouts remained the same. It seemed comical to witness lookouts winking their eyes and motioning to purchasers to move further up whatever street they were operating on that day, and where to pick of whatever drug was needed.

Sellers, and here we are talking about low level conduit suppliers, who were visible and known in the community, were also residing in buildings within the cluster of the projects but not as registered tenants. These sellers, while visible to everyone, were invisible and unaccounted for by the Housing Authority personnel. However, they were known by the Housing Police. It was common knowledge that these low level drug sellers used buildings within the projects to seek transient shelter at many apartments. It was also common knowledge that unregistered tenants were illegally subletting space from legal tenants in federally subsidized housing complexes for monetary gains. This arrangement brought in unaccounted income, which was not reported to the Housing Authority. Money dictated actions.

As the dictum goes, no one knows anything in the projects, and for a host of explanatory reasons such as; prior bad relations with persons of authority within public housing or elsewhere, mistrust of the police, need to survive, lack of opportunity, ignorance, low literacy levels, low expectation, and a culture of instant gratification. Many who were trapped within the projects gave only verbal appreciation of education, yet lacked meaningful participation in the educational process of their children- reports from several sources indicated that it was an exercise in futility getting parents to attend a parent teacher's meeting to discuss issues. Yet the reasons, enumerated in a number of well documented studies on poverty and social conditions, continue to remain sociological and clinical studies, on an ongoing basis, trying to gain a better understanding of the human condition.

R.A. Nisbet, writing in the late 60s, in his book, The Sociological Tradition, said it well. Nisbet like Professor Andrew Hacker, author of Two Nations, concurred in their opinion of choices made by Americans and the difficulties of choice in an ocean of factors. But Nisbet spells out the confusion of ingredients in the pot from which people made daily choices. He stated that on one hand the values of community, moral authority, hierarchy, and the scared must be considered. On the other hand, individualism, equality, moral release, and rationalist techniques of organization and power are the true factors of choice.

This street within the cluster of buildings was a battle zone with daily confrontations between the loiterers, residents, police, and drug dealers whose presence inferred control of each of the four buildings. The control of the buildings belonged, not to the Housing Authority, but to the drug dealers, whose decorum spoke of their commanding grip on activities within each building. Residents were held hostage to the activities on this street while the authorities were exasperated in trying to cut the umbilical cord of illicit activities.

Over time, the known drug dealers were able to distinguish, with precision, whom not to trust, and to decide if entry into the buildings was permissible for persons unknown to them or others in the community. Dealers made door locks malfunction at many buildings and prevented elevators from stopping on certain floors. Entrances to some buildings were blocked. According to housing officials, it became a tiring exercise trying to keep entrances and exit doors functioning. Drug dealers were in total control of these buildings.

After acclimating to the idiosyncrasies of the community, and this took time observing how the residents function, I was minimally prepared to enter the bowels of an environment distant from the known. I learned from pseudo acknowledging of transients, drug dealers, vagrants, and other persons within the buildings, that survival depended upon knowing who the players are in the games of illegal activities when conducting an investigation within the projects. Knowledge became power.

At the assigned apartment, I was greeted at the door by a female who asked to be called Shirley. She informed me the person I was inquiring about was using the bathroom and to wait in the living room. I stood in the living room for what seemed like eternity, waiting for the subject to extricate herself from the bathroom. The investigation had begun.

I did the required checks and determined that the children were in a safe environment. There was sufficient food and appropriate clothing for all family members. Immunizations were current, medical needs were being met appropriately, as was stated on the children's pediatrician report written three days prior to my visit. I was advised by Shirley that a home maker came to the home to assist three days every week. Everything seemed appropriate, until the subject of the investigation appeared.

This tall and overpowering woman announced her presence from the distinctive whiff of alcohol. Her sleepy looking eyes appeared dilated. As I questioned her, I was led to believe that she did not consume alcohol, but habitually ingested a drink called Mussy, which smelt and tasted like beer, but was alcohol free. She even presented an empty bottle of Mussy, while proudly pointing to a six pack chilling in the refrigerator for later in the evening. When I requested her to submit urine samples to be tested for the presence of illicit substances or alcohol, her cordiality ended. Fiery speech followed!

This young woman abruptly ended the conversation. She refused to be screened for alcohol abuse. She also became very agitated, angry, and advised me that BCW would be hearing from her attorney. I left her residence and returned to the field office to seek legal counseling.

Legal consultation and a Child Protective Manager's conference concluded and concurred that the family must be monitored more closely, and any violations would result in removing the children from the mother's care. There were no further demands made upon the birth mother to submit to alcohol or drug screening, while the agency monitoring of the family continued for several months. Due to inconsistencies and social ambiguities in the interpretation and application of the law, the alternative was to monitor.

Legal consultation, on many occasions became continuous wrangling sessions between the legal division and the field office management in the social interpretation of New York Family Law Statutes, and Article 10 sections on Child Protective Proceedings. Since there were two conflicting opinions, the legal division advised that the issue at hand needed a social decision. It was back and forth between managers, legal consultants, and caseworkers with working knowledge of the family's daily functioning. Conferences were reiterations that consumed time in the analysis of imminent risk. Most conferences were simply administrative, indecisive, and minimally productive. The family continued their existence, unencumbered, in the community.

Years later, I made face to face contact with this young mother of five children during a hearing in Family Court. She was then living in another borough without the children in her care. Termination of Parental Rights was in progress. The cycle of TPR repeated itself.

According to her, all the children were removed from her care a few years after my first contact with the family, due to her dependency on alcohol. She appeared to be depressed, nervous, and in a somber mood, as she waited for her appearance before the judge in Family Court.

"I was able to keep it (drinking) a secret for years, believing that I was in control", she confided in a low voice with undertones of embarrassment. "Have you reached out to the agency for assistance with your indulgence?" I inquired "Yea, I went into in-patient at that program up the street, but that was like a vacation and I went through the motions." she replied "I moved from that program to another one, on the advice of a friend, but that didn't work out: I hated the counselor; she behaved like Hitler, rules and more rules! What a bitch she was; did not give you a break, dumb bitch! Oh, the last one I tried, that was a cool program, but I messed up. They were too laid back. I ran the show."

She scratched her head and stated, "I remember now, I can't remember the other one." She continued to enumerate the programs she attended; the list of programs seemed endless. She continued rambling from one subject to another but became specific about her alcohol abuse.

"Those alcohol programs were a joke, everyone was still drinking, including me, but you know how it was, I didn't do anything 24 hours before I pissed in that container." She complained. Brandy's Health's concoctions were at work!

"Look, I visited a friend of mine who had a knee replacement at one of the local hospitals, and we had a ball in his room to celebrate his new knee. You remember Keisha, she was there, and we tore up two bottles of rum, right there." She spoke of that incident in a jovial manner.

"They continue to talk about counseling programs and all that shit that does nothing for me. They know that I was going to have a few drinks here and there, especially on the weekends, but those client conferences, with their appeals, just drove me crazy. They kept going over the same shit all the time. They were behaving like saints-they did not drink; COME ON! I needed a pill or something to control me when I am taking a sip." What comment in a very nonchalant manner!

The cries from these women were piercing, and with amplified tones for help; yet the wanting continued.

All six women in the waiting area were substance abusers who were, in recovery, and traversing numerous programs; under psychotropic medications; under supervision, and had children in their care. All were determined, by their respective clinician, to be stable (?). This conclusion was based on two weekly face-to-face contacts with their social worker or psychiatrist. Supervised field visits also took place; but these visits were perfunctory and for mandated purposes. Because of prior violations with the law, these women either were on parole or on probation; supervised by their respective parole or probation officers, if any. Most had a monthly office-reporting visit and an unannounced home visit monthly. So much for court ordered supervision of clients by staff burdened with expanding caseloads and few resources.

There in plain view, without care about anyone else and very oblivious to the world, they were scheming to gain the upper hand upon the system as the general population refers to government bureaucracy. They were planning to gain public housing in a creative manner by letting the system workers advocate and work in a proactive manner for them. Schemers plan in concert with each other.

"I need a drink after all this planning and whatever, and a good shot of vodka to calm my nerves", a distinctly accented voice in the background bellowed. The accent was Russian. The voice, despite carrying a reminding echo, made me revert to my memory bank to make a connection with the voice.

I peered over the heads of the women in the reception area to allow my ears to connect the accent with a person. I moved closer in the direction of the voice to confirm my suspicions. The female voice, once again, disturbed the silence with a warning that she would not be told what to do by anyone. That utterance was heard years ago, and only from one person; yet it seemed to have been resurrected from the ashes of a time gone by.

To my surprise, seated in the rear were two former clients, male and female. Ellen and Jack became friends here. Both were Eastern European with close Russian, Serbian, and Mongolian ancestry and with Romanian influences. Both were former residents in those countries.

Ellen arrived in the United States as a refugee after the nuclear power plant accident at Chernobyl on April 16, 1986. She was very young with a freshly minted degree in economics in her hand from one of the Ukraine's primary colleges. Accompanying her was Ivor, her son, whose father, Igor, was unaccounted for after the nuclear accident.

Igor, upon graduation from college with Ellen, was fortunate enough to gain employment as an engineer in the Chernobyl reactor. Now he was gone, and Ellen and Ivor had to leave to ensure their survival away from a hostile and unpredictable environment.

Ellen understood limited English upon her arrival in the United States. Yet, despite the language barrier, she was determined to succeed. ESL-English as a Second Language- classes became mandatory on the road to success. She studied vigorously from the text, but pronouncing English was another hurdle. Nevertheless, the challenges were simple reality dealt out to her without any pretension.

That was 1986, almost thirty years ago. Today Ellen's accent remains a variation of the former, but with a lower pitch that deemphasizes the rolling of the tongue; her command of written English was good; but the distinctiveness of her speech pattern made it easy to distinguish from other speakers.

Everything Ellen had was destroyed in the Chernobyl explosion while radioactive particles doomed the faith and hopes for the existence of another generation. People evacuated from Chernobyl in mass exodus, comparable to biblical times. Families were scattered and dislocated throughout Europe while seeking safety and refuge. She spent years trapped in Austria struggling to eke out an existence, while she anticipated the next move.

Ellen traversed Austria to Italy and finally the United States. She made it to the land of opportunity and intended to live the American dream, but with the understanding that there is nothing here, such as a free lunch and that hard work and the deferring of personal satisfaction paves the way for succeeding and that no one owes you anything. It was spelt out in brutal terms of what to expect in America.

Ellen got the message of America. The message was precise and free of ambiguities.

Jack arrived in the United States in 1996. He was 24 years old, and had just graduated from college with a degree in linguistics; he spoke six languages fluently.

Having proficiency in English, a college degree, and good references, Jack applied himself well in the banking sector. He worked his way diligently up the managerial ladder in four years to become supervisor of night operations. Dabbling with bankers, accountants, and business personnel for frequent lunch meetings, became the norm. He would often return to work in a jovial manner, after having several drinks.

It was a job requirement that associating with important clients came with behaviors that were aligned with the client's interest. Conforming to the informal organizational functioning is an implicitly prerequisite for success; while a failure to incorporate aspects of the social interaction, boozing, will have consequences, which can deprive the potential star from climbing the upward mobile ladder of success. Jack fell in line with expectations of the job. He was drinking regularly, as everyone else was doing on the job, but he was drinking excessively on, and off the job as well.

Jack had liquid lunches, as they were termed on Wall Street, but to have a few more after work at the local bar told another story. Jack could not wait until 6pm. Drinks were cheaper in the afternoon. So he, as division head, his day ended at 4:30pm to begin a session of drinking. It became the routine.

At the local bar, patrons seemed to know all the other customers, not only by name, but also by occupation and associations in the financial world. Jack built a good credit base there, which on a monthly basis would exceed $300. Jack was good for the credit; he was earning a good salary.

Jack, like Ellen, had an affinity for vodka. Ellen always said that a good drink was what she needed so that no one can tell her what to do and when. Such were the utterances from Ellen to rationalize having another drink.

But Jack was different in another respect. He anticipated snorting quality cocaine at the end of the day. Almost all colleagues on Wall Street in high stress positions dabbled occasionally with cocaine, as it was described by an associate who worked on Wall Street for over 30 years. Over time, Jack's affinity for cocaine became dependency. Alcohol took a toll on his physical appearance. He paid less attention to the obvious; he rarely shaved, his appearance took a back seat. At times he exhibited boisterous, even lewd, behaviors; things better suited for a saloon.

Ellen, after years of alcohol consumption, was transformed into a compulsive and impulsive abuser of alcohol. Nothing mattered more than the vodka in the bottle, and how to get the next drink. Her quests for the next drink led to indecency; doing what was necessary for the next drink. Her indecency was mechanical and void of emotions, as she whispered sexual phrases with indifference to anyone who was listening. Her approach to solicitation became convoluted to appear as a need, when dependency was ringing the doorbell for fuel. She was prostituting.

Ellen was now in the bowels of dependency and whatever came with it to bring satisfaction to the reward centers in her brain. But there was a darker side to the impact that alcohol was playing in transforming the chemistry of her brain. She had to be fed alcohol.

Ellen related the level to which she was reduced to getting the next bottle of spirits. She was satisfying her own needs and dependency by performing oral; turning tricks. She somehow relied on mental scheduling of male associates (Johns). Most were business owners in the community. Ellen had indeed progressed and transformed to some unknown person.

She stated on a number of occasions that she provided services that were needed. What change of events!

Ellen knew every business owner and her services by word of mouth. She was the tolerated outcast in the community just for her impersonal services, and talked about as the neighborhood drunk. She was seen on a number of occasions staggering on her way to the liquor store after exiting the apartment of one of her regular customers. She had lost everything and herself to the bottle.

In her small community of scattered two family houses, the working class can be easily identified by their bustling early in the mornings to their respective jobs. Ellen would hustle her way along with the working gentry to her next service appointment. Business was good and brisk, especially when city workers were paid. Male workers would indulge in timely oral sex encounters, as a reward for two weeks of toiling. Ellen made a large profit on paydays, but not a fortune.

Ellen completed rehabilitation programs in other communities that had affiliations with local hospitals in the area. At one hospital, she was detoxified more than five times. Other attempts, at detoxification and subsequent counseling sessions, were done at out of state facilities where she was an in- patient. Ellen kept all her appointments with community supportive organizations for alcoholics. She attended AA for over three years then relapsed.

My last contact with Ellen was emotionally charged and filled with empty apologies for failure to take action to improve her quality of existence. Ellen was seeking a referral for a rehabilitation program and housing. She was homeless and drunk.

A year later, Ellen was found in an alley with her pants down and stabbed in the neck.

Jack was on another tract and focused. He completed rehabilitation for cocaine abuse. During his 18 months of rehabilitation, he was never tested positive for cocaine or any other illicit substances. Jack was described by his therapist as exemplary and stable yet he committed suicide with a belt around his neck.

The six women in the waiting area with Ellen made the decision to seek Orders of Protection to set in motion their plan of action. They chose the easiest and most believable of all allegations-domestic violence. The decision was made to file allegations against their male companions.

These women stated, and concurred, that the only avenue to explore was to detail incidents of ongoing domestic violence in the home. In addition, it was agreed that threats of bodily harm to them and their children would become a reality. They knew that because of the high probability of risk of danger, the family would need protection to ensure continued safety for themselves and their children who were in the home.

It was just a perfect plot to begin the process of court actions and to make full use of all services available from the agencies. The strategy began in a coordinated manner, as the group leader detailed the sequence of events. The leader spoke incessantly and laid out detailed plans.

The leader spoke in a knowledgeable manner and with authority as she instructed the other participants on what to do to be granted Orders of Protection. She instructed the other participants to file complaints, with allegations of domestic violence at the local precinct where they lived. The women who lived in each of the five boroughs of the City of New York were instructed to file petitions with the same allegations simultaneously in Criminal and Family Court. It became a two prong approach to demonstrate urgency and the need for judicial intervention to ensure protection for themselves and their children.

According to the group leader, after the plan of action is set in motion, the final step in the process became seeking therapeutic intervention and protection from entities that were financed by private sector donations and grants. These women knew that these organizations advocated in good faith to protect women and children from mental and physical violations. They also knew that domestic violence perpetrated against them, while children remain in the same environment and susceptible to incidents of violence, would trigger immediate actions by all advocacy groups.

These women understood domestic violence as real but failed to understand the seriousness and impact they were having by concocting allegations of abuse. All these individuals understood were a means to an end, and using this avenue for their own gain at the expense of another person's character was something remote to them. The women understood the urgency of responses coming from advocates to protect them and to ensure their safety. They preyed on the good intent of organizations focused on the eradication of domestic violence.

It must be noted that domestic violence, in all its dimensions, needs be confronted with supportive forces of advocacy in the governmental and private sectors, and all members of every society must work forcefully for is eradication. Forces must deal with a cancer from all fronts beginning with, and most necessary, an education.

We, as a nation, must no longer place more emphasis on the cat walk of entertainment or on the football field, and their industries in particular, for financial reasons. Nor should the obsession of the game as entertainment blur the senses to the recognition that physical and psychological damages to women at the hands of actors, entertainers, and sports figures are realities.

Past incidents of alleged domestic violence, perpetrated by Chad Johnson aka Ocho Cinco of Cincinnati Bengals in 2012, and current incidents are growing into concurrency, because it continues to occur with frequency throughout the nation. [15]According to Neil Irwin, New York Times analyst, "domestic violence charges are surprisingly common in the NFL", and are aligned with the general population but is tolerated as exemplified by the leniency of the judicial system to punish.

We know that, like the rest of the population, domestic violence reports are being filed and have been filed against numerous National Football League players such as: Ray Rice, Ravens running back; Adrian Petersen, Vikings running back; Greg Hardy, Carolina Panthers defensive end; Ray Mc. Donald, San Francisco 49ers defensive lineman; Jonathan Dwyer, Arizona Cardinals running back. We also know that the courts were in complicity with the NFL in addressing the issue of domestic violence in a way that exemplified a lack of empathy for the abused, while the abuser was ushered into counseling programs to protect their character, whenever the incident were legally determined to be a felonious offense.

On the one hand, the abuser went into therapy, while the abused got symbols of judicial intervention through the issuance of an Order of Protection. It was known, that anyone, and women in particular, who presented themselves as victims of domestic violence with children in the home, called to action the immediacy for protection from imminent danger. And, there was no question that either court- Criminal or Family- would issue a Temporary Order of Protection until a final determination made the Order good for one year, with a renewable option. A piece of paper- Order of Protection- gave power and access and an early priority selection for housing and other services.

Jackpot!

The next step was the application for public housing.

Getting accepted into public housing was a process entangled with bureaucratic prioritizing and urgency. Names added every day to one of the many already lengthy waiting lists. They were patient and waited for a change in their priority of assigned numbers for years. Other applicants who were victims of domestic violence and were granted court Orders and were receiving intervention services, such as domestic violence counseling or meeting with a psychiatrist on a regular basis, were granted priority by having their names placed in the first tier of applicants for housing. It was that simple for those who were schooled in the arts of exploitation, greed, and obfuscation.

It was common knowledge, gained from and funneled thorough conversation, and based on experience shared by recipients of social entitlement programs that priority allocations for housing were, and are still granted, to persons in domestic violence cases. It was also known and understood that once the need for housing and safety have been established, the conduit for all that the welfare state implies, becomes expansive into every social entitlement program. In such cases, the Federal government, through the Social Security Act of 1935, came alive as it did before, with enduring precedents, that established a new area of Federal responsibility. Social Security continues to address the needs of the indigent, those less fortunate, and in need of assistance.

After 18 months of court ordered supervision of Andrew, a good relationship, based on trust, developed. He was an abuser which demanded a different understanding of addiction and dependency. Therefore I decided to use the tools of psychology, academic theories, research and related techniques to enter the bowels of the addicted with empathy, not sympathy.

They all received the typical new court order: random alcohol and drug screening, monitoring compliance with all the programs requirements, and follow up reports to the Court. All three were back into the revolving doors of mandated rehabilitation programs. However, this time there was a twist: follicle testing. The latter testing method, which was quite costly, had been ordered for numerous clients whose behaviors and violations of mandates, whether it was failure to report to a parole officer or probation officer, necessitated this approach to ensure compliance. Follicle testing to the drug addict or alcoholic was like a death sentence; they were faced with conclusive proof of their continuous indulgences and there was no way of escaping, evading, or disingenuously obfuscating the truth.

When the old country was discussed, Lewis always emphasized his place of residence and affinity to the Big Apple. According to him, he was grounded here, with no other place to go, because he had been acculturated for the past 50 years to New York City and understood its' complexities. Lewis, on a number of occasions, like many, referred to the years spent in New York City as the assimilation to the dregs, because for him anything goes, once it does not interfere with him, he would continue to live. Lewis saw himself as a true New Yorker.

None of the participants were progressing to sobriety. They stopped making efforts, beyond perfunctorily adhering to programs' stipulations, while using methods to evade the next drug screening test. The cycle of their involvement with substances continued. I subsequently learned that Andrew and Lewis, who were congregating in the neighborhood park, were killed by stray bullets as rivaling gangs were shooting at each other.

THE PROBLEM

A great percentage of clients whom I supervised were under court orders, and with the stipulation that a rehabilitation program was mandatory. It seemed odd that clients, who understood the implications of their actions, would violate the court's order and make themselves vulnerable to the edicts of the courts. However, the behavior was, as expected, when looked at carefully.

Clients knew and accepted their addiction and dependency. Clients also knew and accepted their continuum of involvement in rehabilitation programs as part of the process, but were only committed to the detoxification phase. They shared the common belief that detoxification cleanses the body of drugs and would be used as a period of respite from further indulgences.

Clients confessed to using programs as a recess period away from any indulgences. They also accepted and prattled the phrase that relapse was part of recovery as gospel truth on a conscious level. Clients regurgitated, "I'm a recovering addict", and repeated this utterance, when appeals for assistance were sought. They also understood, how and when to make an appeal to the human instinct to extend a helping hand, whenever they demanded assistance.

Most abusers felt trapped with the continuum of programs doing the same things and going through the same phases. Many of those who completed all phases of rehabilitation felt that they were prepared to function independently of any support system. Many felt frustrated with the same repetitive questions at every new intake when their record and history spoke for itself. Most clients felt angry at having to reiterate past issues, which they felt, were gone and should be buried and left untouched.

One abuser took things a step further. This client was ingenuous at being prepared for the intake process by having a documented list of diagnoses at hand. It was his belief that being prepared made the clinician's work less complicated while alleviating the stressful effects of reiterations. He recognized the failure of clinicians to be prepared, and attributed their failure to larger and demanding caseloads.

Most deviated from any structure because of their new sense of independence. Despite the great majority failing to maintain a continuum of sobriety, they retained an ingrained skill at manipulating bureaucrats through their ongoing appeals for assistance. Bureaucrats were trapped by Federal, State and City directives and mandates into extending different kinds of help. It became a vicious effort not only for the abusers who carried the weight of survival, but also for those who provided the intervention between the influencing forces to impede further indulgences. Workers were caught in a bind trying to provide the required services needed while adhering to mandates.

Simply put, workers had to synergize their efforts with the courts, and many rehabilitation programs and clinicians to adhere to mandates. Workers were also expected to attend numerous families and school conferences, while updating documentation to avoid law suits. Workers were reprimanded by supervisors and gossiped about by colleagues. They were bogged down with documenting information instead of providing what was necessary to address a particular situation. Their assignments became documenting to avoid the next litigation and this took a greater part of their workday. It was required and implicitly, throughout the agency, known as CYA (cover your ass), to prevent internal battles which can become litigious and subsequently costly to the agency. Because of these requirements and timeframes, seemingly written in stone, it became compromising the mission of extending a helping hand.

The agency evolved only to categorize, dissect, and compartmentalize into a theoretical framework services that only addressed the clinical issues on paper. It was the ongoing and recreating what was termed protocols, coupled with evidence-based approaches, and promising preventive programs, with new definitions to address real issues. This was accomplished by using crisis management techniques, and division of labor principles.

However, on closer examination, these efforts were duplicitous where services overlapped, and provided by numerous titled consultants and specialists. It was whimsical to hear intervention approaches with titles like Multi Systemic Therapy, Functional Family Therapy, and Brief Strategic Family Therapy. The list will continue with variations of approaches to address the same issues in changing times.

All these requirements were mandatory, while workers had to adhere to training sessions for nothing more than compliance, and preparing perfunctory reports that reiterated the known and monitoring clients who were changing residences constantly. As workers were burdened with these tasks, new departmental heads continued to micro manage to satisfy their egos. Most of the time workers had to leave or defer documentation for a later time, and this could be delayed for days or weeks. It was common to see workers struggling to adhere to directives while trying to advocate effectively for clients whose needs changed constantly.

In addition, the most difficult task for the interventionist, while adhering to all the directives, was the building of trust in dysfunctional families where inconsistency and unreliability were part of their functioning. This task demanded a fluidity of sorts between clients and workers and this took time and effort to develop. Although management understood that without a good working relationship between client and worker, the objectives of the agency would be extremely difficult and exasperating to attain, workers were implicitly directed to pay specific attention to documentation and to relegate other aspect of their assignment to secondary importance. Families were, and continue to be, the mission of the agency.

It seemed that the thrust and most important aspect of workers assignment were children and families. Yet the verbal demands for accurate documentation to avoid litigation were loud, as the invisible warning card with headlines in the local press hung over the heads of workers. The job dictated documentation. It was the continuous grind for each worker to master, as was said before, the art of CYA (cover your ass) so that the agency appeared, on paper, as fulfilling their mandate. The public knew better, through ongoing litigation, that bureaucracies, like ACS, were a spectacle of inefficiency and poor management, in cases like Jessica Cortez in 1989, Nixzmary Brown in 2006, Marchella Brett-Pierce in 2010, and Myles Dobson in 2014, and dozens of other mismanaged cases.

I say this, most agencies are driven by services and not by results and are less focused on efficiency or management analysis of the environment in which they function. Agencies are about training and rote learning and not educating workers to engage in inductive and deductive reasoning. It was an ongoing practice for workers to be summoned to a training session that interrupted everything that was being addressed to satisfy requirements. Many sessions were nothing but reiterations that consumed productive time or presentations of little value. It was a world that was consumed with conferences and guest speakers, unplanned union meetings, memos that made little sense, and spontaneous mini meetings whenever a crisis erupts.

Management by crisis was the ongoing theme in layered filled bureaucracies with duplicitous positions of authority. It continues.

THE THOUGHT

After more than two decades in city government, with various responsibilities within the Department of Social Services, and ten years in the private sector, an understanding of each sector's philosophical approach to the human condition developed. This understanding came from witnessing the approaches, attitudes, behaviors, and responsibilities of personnel in both sectors.

The private sector rewards for creativity and talent while inefficiency is punished. The public sector continues to strive for economic equality by spending, without accountability, and manages by crisis. Inefficiency in the public sector is not punished but implicitly encouraged by reassigning personnel through lateral appointments with newly minted titles that have little relevance to the assignment at hand. The public sector has become a mill of titles to obfuscate what one really does within the title. Everyone has a title, created by expansive social needs, to symbolize a leap forward in meeting the needs of the less fortunate.

[16]Alexis de Tocqueville came to America in 1831, and he described his journey as trying "to unravel the secrets to success of a fledgling nation that was already competing with powers of Europe" and to try to make sense of the new system of government that was succeeding. In 1835, he noticed, as expansion of social needs continued, and with the trust to make conditions equal, the more people resented the inequalities that remain. This paradox of equality, in all its phases, whether it is gender or finances, then promotes and fosters feelings of envy by pitting both sectors against each other- Tocqueville was right.

This understanding of both sectors ultimately led to the conclusion that if both entities are to survive as viable and autonomous and with different approaches for providing assistance, the core trust of extending governmental assistance must be grounded in cost-benefit analysis and financial outcomes. Budgets must be based on affordability and grounded in economics so that opinions on assistance are not filled with emotional thinking and void of financial realities. There must be an understanding of how resources are allocated efficiently and effectively at all levels.

This does not infer that altruism is dead. Rather, it would remain the centerpiece for extending a helpful hand to those in need. Helping the indigent must remain a mandate for all sectors of the population. Therefore, the concept of just helping, because of empathy and a desire to help, without a clear understanding of the implications of financial accountability, further promotes the inequalities. Bureaucracies breed and feed upon the misallocating resources through inefficiency. Agencies are always in crisis management status trying to reinvent the wheel through new rules and regulations without creativity to maximize the extension of help to the indigent.

Then the responsibilities for helping those in need must be left to the charities whose mission propels the extending of assistance through fundraising and tax abatements. Leading charities such as Catholic and Jewish philanthropies (Tzedakah), and the Salvation Army, are organizations, among others, that have clearly demonstrated their abilities to use modern financial tools to provide assistance. These organizations understand the role of management and their responsibilities in using resources efficiently.

In other words, the financing for those in need must be gained from value taxation and designed in a cost benefit manner to establish a report of accountability for the taxpaying public. Therefore, budgetary allocations must be contingent on positive outcomes resulting from new approaches and creative thinking.

To arrive at this goal, management in the public sector must encourage new approaches and thinking to come from the regular members workers. Too often directives coming from the upper echelons of management are cast into a text book approach detailing steps to follow which are incongruous with reality. Let workers think.

In the public sector, when examined carefully, most persons in management positions are trained and not educated in management. Training only brings about what was taught. It fails to recognize new approaches by lower level workers who must follow directives blindly. We must move away from the psychological and sociological thinking of helping because that is the, "mission of the agency" to helping without accountability to "save one life". Management and social thinking must converge so that the public is presented with accountability at all levels.

There must also be room for workers to tap into their own creative self to attain the set goals of their work, while keeping the mission of the agency the focus. If the goal can be attained by using the matrix of efficiency and effectiveness, then the manual of operations can remain simply academic for guidance and not a rigid and inflexible set of guidelines. Let the informal organizational approach to solving problems become a reality.

Simply put, let the creative approach of workers mean something. Give workers latitude in attaining the mission of the agency.

OBSERVATIONS

During my tenure in social services, requests for assistance were an ongoing daily activity. After a holiday weekend, assistance varied from the personal to families in need of intervention. Seeking assistance was not confined to the indigent or the abused or the psychological impaired; everyone sought help in one form or another.

A large percentage of people seeking help deserved assistance, but the problematic few, who are using the system to gain the upper hand by demanding services, must be accountable through entitlement reforms. Those gaming the system were using known tools, and in this case children, and its appendage- dependency- to fortify their claims and need for assistance.

Clients came to the field office demanding assistance for children. Later abandoning the same children for whom benevolent requests appeased their senses. Others just reached out to the agency for referrals to rehabilitation programs for substance abusers. It was an eclectic pool of applicants with backgrounds from a doctor who lost her medical license to school teachers seeking intervention for students to a former chemist in need of drug rehabilitation. Some applicants for assistance remained indelible from the acts they committed on a revolving basis.

I recall vividly having difficulties in making face-to-face contact with a birth mother at the address provided in the oral report from the State Central Registry. Just as I concluded that all attempts at making contact with the birth mother were exhausted, I was summoned to the front desk to meet with a client who refused to provide her name but knew that I was her assigned worker. The client, according to the security guard, had in her possession a handful of agency stationery, business cards, and notification letters, but refused to provide her names. Rather she demanded to be seen by me. Who could this be?

Before going to the reception area, the security guard warned me that the client appeared to be a "bag lady "or "homeless" from her appearance. She was reported to speaking in monotones and her speech was disjointed in a rambling manner.

The female client was an obese female standing at military attention clinching two large shopping bags filled with her belongings. She appeared disheveled and her body odor was repugnant to the senses- she smelt like rotten apples.

We exchanged pleasantries. She spoke with an air of authority and had a command of each subject that she was speaking about, but in a very disjointed manner. She quoted Alexander Pushkin, a Russian author of the Romantic era, considered the greatest Russian poet. Pushkin's matrilineal great grandfather, Abram Gannibal, was a page slave that was kidnapped and brought from Africa to Russia as, a gift for Peter the Great. She spoke of Vladmir Pozner, born in France and grew up in America until eighteen then moving to the Soviet Union in 1952. She referred to Pozner as the only person who truly understood both societies because he lived in both and spoke their different languages. She then shifted the conversation to Mark Twain and American writers. She abruptly stopped talking and looked directly into my eyes with a piercing and a thoughtful look and stated:

"My students did this to me, they collaborated, have you spoken to my psychiatrist? I am Dr. -------- let him know I'm here", she uttered while glancing at the adjacent wall and thrusting her body forward to prepare herself for engagement in dialogue. "I would suggest you get in contact with my psychiatrist and let him know I'm here." As she continued speaking, her hands rummaged through her belongings looking for a business card. At last, she retrieved it from between stacks of other cards that were wrapped in a discolored handkerchief. The chalk white business card with black raised lettering was creased, discolored, and looked frayed.

I looked at the card and recognized the physician's name. On a prior occasion, consultations with this clinician proved worthy; he was skillful and knowledgeable in providing assistance and guidance in understanding some incongruous behaviors. I immediately called his office, as requested by Dr. -----, the name the client called herself. I also faxed a release of confidential information to his office and waited for a phone call from the psychiatrist. He returned my call after receiving the signed release, which is mandatory protocol.

The psychiatrist verified that the client was indeed a physician who had lost her license to practice medicine. I subsequently learned that this non-licensed and non- practicing physician was censored due to drugs and alcohol abuse. She lost her practice; she lost her children; she lost herself to psychiatric problems. She was seeking assistance, which came too late- a drug overdose was her end.

I also recall, a former client, who was one of the most honest, but manipulative individuals, who used the in-patient detox center, as a precursor to access out- patient services for housing and additional help. He always, like his decease woman, wanted a good team of professionals to be proactive in advocating on their behalf. He did his research well on most programs to ensure that both of them, whenever there was a need for detoxification, was in the best facility - such was his modus operandi.

He was in more in more detoxification units than he was able to recall, and at different phases of drug rehabilitation. He entered detoxification and attended outpatient clinics in numerous cities throughout the country, but was always apprehensive to seek intervention where the population mix reflected the lower class. A few years ago, he made a conscious decision, as he had done in the past, to try something different. As I mentioned he always did his research, but this time he was exploring assistance at well-funded programs that caters to all in need of spiritual healing. This was uncommon for him, but he felt an inner voice speaking to him that help must come with a spiritual connection. For some unknown reason, he connected with a higher being. intermittent contact with whoever presented himself or herself as involved with the power of the Spirit. May his soul be at rest!

A little bit on Baddas, as I called him, so you can get to understand his inner workings. He used heroin, methadone, cocaine, numerous pain medications, and enjoyed smoking marijuana whenever he was encouraged to indulge. Strangely enough, he would smoke marijuana but would not contribute financially to make a purchase. On the other hand, he would be the first to pull money out of his pocket if the purchase was for heroin or cocaine. He saw marijuana not as an herb placed on earth for all to use.

He would be the first to confess that he was an addict and that all efforts at rehabilitation by him were temporary and reverting to his old self was something beyond his control. On many occasions, he would declare that there had to be something else beyond the standard approaches to drug rehabilitation, but he had not stumbled upon it yet. Baddas wanted to stop using illicit drugs, but knew that stopping with the aid of psychotherapy sessions was less than helpful; Baddas received numerous psychiatric interventions over his more than two decades of indulgences.

He attributed his behaviors to chemical imbalances in his brain. He refrained from divulging his diagnosis, if any. Baddas divulged little of himself beyond indicating a strained relationship with his parents. He was married three times and divorced twice but kept an amicable relationship with his former wives.

On one occasion, Baddas called after a long absence. I heard him panting for breath on the phone as spoke rapidly while stating his dilemma. He had just completed ten days of detoxification, and was being discharged in an hour. He was penniless and was in a hurry. He requested my assistance to convert the vouchers he given to him at discharge into cash. That was the problem!

The two vouchers were valued $10. He also needed to convert his monthly food allocation from SNAP valued $130 into cash. That was another problem! I heard the urgency in his voice, and it dictated compromise. The compromise in this case was to convert and discount his SNAP for $100 and vouchers for $5. He was illegally discounting a benefit.

Baddas saw this arrangement as bartering and good for everyone. It was not a big issue for him because knew it as a common occurrence in almost every neighborhood. He knew that there were discounting agents for SNAP stipends at the local mom and pop stores in every neighborhood. Being an enabler was out of the question since there was no working relationship with any individual who conducted that type of business.

He asked if it was a good time for him to stop by the office. Since that day's schedule had an opening of a few hours, we agreed to meet.

He was one of those clients who was very amicable, and had an inner quality that transcended into an appeal for help without him having to express a desire or a need. Baddas was smart; knowledgeable of biblical issues and well versed in street pharmaceuticals.

Baddas was lucky to be accepted for another round of detoxification at the local hospital. Lucky, because new budget appropriations for detoxification were limited in all of the country and he knew that. Since things were changing everywhere, his planning had to be precise.

Baddas arrived at my office within an hour. He was well dressed and clean shaven. He gained weight; he admitted to eating too much during his ten day stint in detoxification and being lethargic. His body language told the story for his visit; he seemed anxious.

"How's it going? What's up these days, brother?" I inquired.

"I need a drink, but a hit would be nice," Baddas stated. He opened his right hand revealing a small plastic bag filled with white pills.

I immediately questioned Baddas about the origin of the pills and advised him about the legal implications for possession of a controlled substance. He gave a deaf ear to all that I saying. He was only thinking about the pills.

Before his admission into detox, he scouted the environment within the boundaries of the hospital looking for a safe location to store his recently purchased pain killers. He made the purchase at one of the many illicit drug supermarkets throughout the city. Baddas was known in the circles of illicit drug activities and transactions and was warmly received during purchases from reliable dealers whose products were of consistent quality, whether it was for heroin or painkiller medications. At the drug supermarket sales of marijuana were not allowed and dealers saw very little incentive or profits from selling marijuana.

Baddas, once again, entered detoxification disingenuously to accomplish his mission. This was nothing new for him and others who used detoxification, as the buffer, when funds were short and they were unable to afford to purchase the quantity of pain killers that were needed for the remainder of the month. Baddas was addicted to pain killers and dependent on alcohol, and habitually used his monthly allocation of SNAP funds in a few days. For the remainder of the month he borrowed from friends and associates to supplement his wants for pain killers.

For some unexplained reason he failed to complete recertification in the required time for SNAP funds. Because he had exhausted his borrowing limits, entering detoxification became the only choice and another avenue that was used by addicts, like him, to get pain medications. It is known among addicts that pain medications- Suboxone, Buprenorphine, Benzodiazepines, and anti-nausea medications are given to those who are in detoxification by staff to alleviate pains resulting from withdrawals. In cases like that, those who voluntarily entered detox were only there to satisfy their thirst for narcotics, as a therapy, and cost free and legally administered.

Baddas hid his stuff in a place that was guaranteed safe and free of foot traffic. He wanted his stash of painkillers to be easily accessible upon his discharge. He felt relieved from tension when he noticed no parking signs were posted on both sides of the street, and would remain in effect for the next two weeks. These signs gave comfort to Baddas because he knew that vagrants would not be around to steal his precious goods.

He checked into the detoxification unit but his mind could not think of anything else but the pills. He could not wait for discharge to get his hands on pills.

Baddas was discharged ten days later and he immediately rushed to the secret location. He retrieved his hidden stash. Luck was on his side; his pouch of Vicodin pills was intact despite the weather. He was pleased.

Eight months later a voice on the telephone grunted, "I can't do this anymore. I am forty years old today and at the bottom of the pit with shit all over me" he was out of breath. I continued listening. There was total silence for what seemed like eternity. "Yo, do you hear me.?" He shouted.

"I hear you. What do you want to do?" I asked. "To be away for a long time and this is the time and I'm ready," he stated.

A few weeks later Baddas called. He was in a residential program 300 hundred miles from his home. He described the facility as great and well organized with the best clinical staff and spiritual leaders. According to Baddas, it was a "God send with caring people". His sojourn lasted 9 months. There was no contact for those months.

As usual, before the holidays to celebrate Passover, I would visit friends in the community to extend my wishes. On one of the holy days in question, I was summoned by an associate to perform a commissioners' duty at a local business. According to my associate, all the required documents had been prepared and photocopied were placed into different colored envelopes. My duties were to verify signatures, check identifications, and have witnesses present. I packed my working tools- recording book, seal, and commissioners stamp- and headed to the location.

It was a store front with plastered signs on the outside advertising things from cooked food to stationery. As I entered, I heard several voices speaking, laughing, shouting, and an intermitting outburst that silenced the other participants. Tolerable music was playing in the back ground.

A burly man stood attention at the entrance with an intimidating look as he watched. I moved further into the storefront. No words were spoken but glances were exchanged among the gathering.

"Here to meet with your boss or the person in charge" was my introduction. The goons moved closer in as if they were going to spring into an attack. Their decorum had a chilling effect. The place was silent. All eyes looked in my direction as a head emerged from the gathering-it was Baddas with a glass of alcohol in one hand and a joint in the other.

"What can I tell you, only live and let live. I need something more than a program," he stated. Baddas was once more appealing for sympathy.

Our last contact was in an arena with humans, who knew a better way, and had a choice to make, but remained indifferent while consciously rationalizing their ongoing behaviors. Baddas committed the ultimate act five months later at his father's residence; a needle stuck in his arm.

To understand the behaviors and choices of the so-called indigent population seeking relief and assistance, one must understand the genesis of their manipulations and its properties, and all the factors that contribute to their current state of being. The addict will be an addict traveling for his next fix without consideration for anything else but the immediate satisfaction by any means necessary.

THE LEXICON

Alcoholics, drug addicts, and others of dependency, once engaged in rehabilitation programs, voluntarily or involuntarily, become automatons and believers and disciples of what was thought. These participants, without examination or question, have inculcated into their daily lives the known responsive phrase in recovery, which becomes the mantra. This phrase (in recovery) is universally known, recognized and prattled as a badge of honor by a large percentage-80%- of those seeking avenues for recovery and sobriety. The other 20%, although participants in rehabilitative programs have verbally declared that being in recovery, as an ongoing process, concludes when the goal of sobriety has taken root. When the goal has taken root, the new lexicon emerges silently and evolves to have recovered.

Every person in all known rehabilitation programs are taught, and ascribe to the in recovery dogma with conviction and without prejudice. This is reinforced by repetitive usage and acceptance that is supported by experts in the field of addiction. This implies that people in recovery see the process as protracted into infinity. It also acknowledges that recovery is a process over time with no known end.

What is not being considered throughout the recovery process is the role being played on the intellect of the addict when he or she, if defined as such, uses the phrase in recovery. The addict while in the rehabilitative process finds it difficult to disassociate from in recovery and have as its replacement the theme have recovered with support. The addict becomes one with the phrase, without examining the content behind the phrase, and hence the rote process of learning is reinforced with dissatisfaction, while struggling for change and freedom from what led to the dependency continues. Recovery then becomes a revolving door of ongoing programs and no actual progression. You have the right to take the next hit.

If indeed, the alcoholic and others of dependency are in [17] "the phenomenon of dissatisfaction", as Dr. Frederick S. Perl clearly stated, and then the dissatisfaction with oneself and functioning becomes the basis for change as stated in Gestalt Therapy Verbatim. Change then becomes possible.

Thus, if dissatisfaction with oneself becomes the driving force for change of self and the environment, then let us change from the implied continuum of recovering by using language to reflect a more positive reference to oneself in the healing process. Recovered then becomes the new mantra.

THE LEXICON AT WORK

All substance abusers, despite indulging in stupid behaviors, are very skillful and bright and have good insight into how to make the system, as in social services, work for them in meaningful ways. It is known by those seeking assistance that persons in the helping professions are susceptible to pleas for help because of their empathetic nature and desire to extend a helping hand, especially to those who are engaged with rehabilitation efforts. They also knew how to use what had been taught in rehabilitation programs, and to apply this newly acquired knowledge to manipulate the empathetic nature of those with whom they have established a good client relationship, whether it is pseudo or perfunctory.

Their command and use of the preposition combined with the noun into the phrase, in recovery, and the active phrase recovering have become their catch phrases when pleading for help. For the alcoholic and drug addict the mastery in soliciting assistance of various kinds becomes a compelling art that impels the human instinct to empathize. Abusers understood in their own way and how the rights to services, as stipulated by federal mandate, can be extended to them when they apply such terms in begging for assistance. They understood that whatever agency they had to work with also subscribes to the goal of stability for client.

Each client, who was in a recovery program, uttered verbatim the phrase in recovery as an appendage to his or her daily existence. It appeared that the phrase remained dominant in every aspect of their daily lives, and in recovery would preface every statement as a tool to gain sympathy and empathy in a very conscious and deliberate manner. They remained skillful!

At all helping profession agencies, it became the here and now approach, with assistance to prevent the placement of children in foster care. Assistance varied from purchasing food to last for a few days until SNAP funding is activated, or to the recertification and subsequent approval so that families can qualify for what was termed the one shot deal or emergency food stamps. In a few cases, clients understood that going through the motions are prerequisites that gives them immediate access to meager cash funding, and at the same time, prepares them for long term assistance. On many occasions, the agency would purchase beds, furniture, and clothing for children. This assistance was provided through emergency funds that are needed so that clients can address their immediate needs and that of their families.

Clients also understood the importance and the usage of key words or phrases like domestic violence, dangerous living conditions, or imminent risk, during the intake process, and how it would become the conduit to adequate housing and other benefits. Requests for one-time payments to assist with gas and electric bills, and rental were ongoing. Some clients alleged possible eviction unless arrears in rent were paid promptly. It was cheaper than having the family evicted and housed in a city shelter. It remained intervention and management by crisis.

Many clients were conspiring with unscrupulous property owners to fleece governmental agencies of badly needed funds. The proprietor and tenant shared and benefited from stipends provided by agency assistance. Clients would also detail stressors affecting their ability to address their own needs and that drug and alcohol problems are affecting their lives.

A number of clients were very knowledgeable of social services mandates for assistance. They knew how much money would be given immediately to them to prevent placement of their children in the foster care system. It was not much, but enough to buy alcohol and drugs. Extending assistance became tedious and never ending.

Yes, the clients were cognitively attuned of their dependency as functional addicts and that they needed whatever substances they were using in order to function. Yet, they remained in programs for years while surrendering to perfunctory modalities just to exist. Certainly, clients, as was said earlier, were not stupid, but many were highly functional in the arts of manipulation for their personal gains. Or could it be that clients understood some aspect of their addiction not recognized by clinicians.

These behaviors can be called manipulation and symptomatic of addiction and dependency, but it does not explain the client who is experiencing the dilemma of the twin issues of addiction and dependency. Those clients, who remained in the continuum of recovery programs, demonstrated behaviors, which inferred new needs that were satisfied by social services agencies. The client looked forward to the next handout.

THE GAME

The thrust of additional governmental assistance is rooted in rehabilitation programs, which are prerequisites, or qualifying conditions for extending help through SNAP. The focus of treatment continues to attribute all emotional and behavioral problems of a client to the use of alcohol and drugs and with an emphasis at addressing psychological issues. This approach keeps the physiological component, the main culprit, on the back burner despite recent research showing that physiology plays the dominant and significant role in addiction and alcoholism.

A great percentage of addicts and alcoholics, who were in different phases of rehabilitation, stated to me that they would simply acquiesce to whatever the recommendation and intervention services may be, just to appease the clinician. It became known as, going through the motions, as clients say, to satisfy the agency's requirements for rehabilitation or a court mandate. The agency sets standards to be upheld and adhered to by the client. The client, on the other hand, does not have any power, and as such, acquiesces to the established standards. Therefore, clients must adhere to the one fits all standards and rules.

These interventions, according to clients, were not intended to determine causation of addiction and dependency. Rather, the approaches used by counselors and therapists were a little Sigmund Freud, a little Gestalt; a little RET and maybe Rogers. These interventions were seen by clients as common psycho socials of information gatherings sessions that concurred with the medical director's treatment plan which would keep or help them to remain stable. The approach, through lectures on addiction and on the disease concepts of alcoholism, and alcoholism itself were also seen as the building blocks of information that would eventually lead to the goal of sobriety. Then the question becomes, when?

Most clients were treated on an outpatient basis, known as the real world approach whereby clients lived in their respective neighborhoods, received telephone and face-to-face contacts, and attended weekly group sessions. Clients stated that the regimentation of weekly group sessions were seen as nothing more than reinforced reminders of what they were already taught and knew about their addiction. Such contacts were seen as reality checks to keep them from complacency.

These therapies were administered by LCSW and MSW certified counselors who worked tirelessly with abusers in an effort to make whatever progress may be possible. Rather, it appeared unintentionally, due to litigation and mandates that the only real focus continues to be functional stability of the client, while using the modalities described in their current DSM to apply the art of psychoanalyzing. I will speak more about the current DSM5 published in 2013 in a later chapter.

Many habitual clients of conscious recidivism in rehabilitation programs stated that they were in control of the process of soliciting and gaining assistance by using the vehicle and tools of the psychotherapeutic community. The application of their tools begins at the intake stage with the case worker who initiates the process of referrals to other clinicians who do the analysis and attaches a clinical label. Once the client receives the clinical labels, the process continues.

Remember, in recovery, is the theme within the label that defines the behavior.

The DSM 5

Clinicians and those working in the helping professions do attach, from analysis and observation and research, descriptive labels to categorize behaviors, and then fit the labels neatly into psychiatric definitions. According to Dr. Leonard Sax, psychologist, and here he is referring to the old 2012 DSM (Diagnostic Statistical Manual), there was time when specifics mattered when, "the patient had to meet certain specific criteria in order to be diagnosed for any particular condition" before the label was attached. Therefore, symptoms had to be specific such as delusions or hallucinations.

From about 1940 to 1970, Sigmund Freud's theoretical concepts of mental life and its disorders dominated American psychiatry. Freud believed and stated "important facts about our mental life are disguised, buried in the unconscious, and stifled by convention and conformity". During that period Freud and his followers did not see or make the connection between family background, education, occupation, intelligence, temperament, habits, and medical condition as being important enough to play as significant or dominant role in mental health. Yet, members of the profession realized that very little progress was being made by their patients, who were treated, using Freudian approaches, while medications like lithium showed some progress in treating severe mental disorders. Clinicians began to change their focus by looking for alternative approaches to treat their patients.

It was during that same period, I recall, hearing of Cognitive Behavioral Therapy- teaching patients how to live with their problems to the best of their abilities. As an alternative way to treating the person, Cognitive Behavioral Therapy approached the issue of mental illness with a twist. CBT requires taking an active role and knowing oneself and to be prepared in the truest sense. Simply know yourself intimately. At that time, I began to explore writings by Carl Rogers, B.F. Skinner, Frederick S. Perls M.D., Ph.D. and others in the field of CBT.

At that, time professionals focused on treating mental illness as disorders of the unconsciousness. Theories were everyday occurrences and everyone was on the bandwagon coming up with new approaches. But nothing made real sense to add to bits and pieces of findings by professionals, who seemed to be drowning themselves in personal opinions of mental illness and addiction. Everyone had an opinion, and differing too.

The evolution of ideas and opinions has now changed progressively, and really! The change that has taken place has now accommodated room for new thinking. However, this new thinking has set in motion the loosening of rules in an ambiguous style, by leaving interpretation to the individual clinician, and this leaves room for guessing to fit the defined rules.

Today, according to Dr. McHugh, professor of Psychiatry at Johns Hopkins Hospital, the client has become much attuned to the rote interpretations of mental illness by health care professional and stated, "the public complains that psychiatrists seem ready to call every state of mental distress an illness", and "the public is not far wrong". This then leads to interpretations dissimilar as two painters painting a picture of the same object.

Because of the loosening of rules filled with ambiguities, adherence to the new thinking makes it difficult to say how the process works and tedious to think of the process at work. Nevertheless, it has now become the Babel of clinical feelings all wrapped up in empathy for the client that ultimately traps the client into the assistance syndrome, while they are engaging an advocate in the psychotherapeutic community. I call this involuntary enabling of the client.

The loosening of rules is clearly spelt out in the [1] DSM5 of 2014. Appearing is the DSM-5, are pages 66, 122, and 708, which broadsides ones cognitive capacity, to the point where the word "unspecified" becomes incomprehensible and meaningless. We are now talking about "Unspecified Schizophrenia Spectrum Disorder" and "Unspecified Attention Deficit/ Hyperactivity Disorder and Unspecified Mental Disorder".

The aforementioned, unspecified categories, has as the only requirement for a determination is that you "do not meet full criteria for any mental disorder." In other words, you are behaving or acting in a manner to infer incongruous behaviors. Page 66 in the DSM 5 specifically stated that no criterion has to be present and that "occasional symptoms of inattention" which causes "significant distress or impairment" becomes the basis for an unspecified disorder. Something mentally has occurred but ambivalence and apprehension shifts from a diagnosis.

It is no wonder that [20] Dr. Allen Frances, psychiatrist and professor emeritus at Duke University School of Medicine, refers to the new DSM 5 as Cosmetic Psychiatry where there is "the creating inflation in psychiatric diagnosis" and "an explosion in the use of expensive, often unnecessary, and harmful psychotropic drugs". We have certainly seen in our communities, read in the media, and are aware of the effects upon children treated with Adderall, and Ritalin, which are harmful psychotropic drugs that manifest its dangerous side later.

In March 2013 the Federal Centers for Disease Control and Prevention in Atlanta, Georgia, released data showing that [21]11% of school-age children in the U.S- 6.4 millions- had received a medical diagnosis of attention-deficit hyperactivity disorder, a 41% increase in the past decade and more than two-thirds received Adderall or Ritalin. This rise in numbers of children treated with Adderall and Ritalin started the debate of children being over diagnosed and overmedicated for ADHD. The ballooning in medications is due to Cosmetic Psychiatry diagnosis gaining popularity. This new diagnosis in conjunction with marketing strategies by global pharmaceutical companies to direct the psychotherapeutic community to seek undefined categorization of symptoms, as now spelt out in the DSM5, is troubling. This new practice of psychiatric diagnosis is not limited to the U.S, but has now taken root globally.

A look at Israel in 2010 shows [22] nearly one in five Israeli children were diagnosed with ADHD and prescribed Ritalin and/ or Concerta. In Saudi Arabia there is an ADHD Society that is solely sponsored by the Belgian company Janssen. On its website, they promote the use of both medications. In China and South Korea, because of the push for academic excellence, and the extended hours spent on rote learning, cramming, and studying to master subjects, children have trouble coping with such stress, resulting in poor behavior and performance. ADHD medications have been have become the answer to restore focus and control.

Currently the worldwide sales of ADHD medications escalated to $14 billion in just two years, in a greater part because of the loosening of rules and the lack of defining what constitutes a real diagnosis that is free of subjectivity. As Dr. Allen Frances rightfully pointed out "the inflation of psychiatric diagnosis" will lead to newly minted labels.

Cosmetic psychiatry has taken root and has moved into a circle of nonsense. Cosmetic psychiatry aborts Normal grief for the new classification as Major Depressive Disorder. Because of a new label or name, [20] "pills and medical rituals will be applied to a person's natural emotional reaction to the loss of a love one", according to numerous well established psychiatrists. The new titles specifically say that humans are not allowed to grieve and experience normal biological reaction to loss and must be labeled as having a disorder. Because of the new label/diagnosis, and by extension, creates the incentives for drug companies to promote and endorse drugs only for profits.

Let us look at the newly minted diagnosis, and with a grain of salt.

Forgetfulness will now be labeled as Minor Neurocognitive Disorder. A temper tantrum, when displayed by a child, he or she would now be diagnosed as Disruptive Mood Dysregulation Disorder. Once again, we see the application of an art and not science to differentiate human behaviors, interpreted to fit the clinicians, bent of thinking.

The clinician does not stop at just labeling. Rather, the clinician reflexively, not because of new thinking, but because of the choices from the vast array of newly minted diagnosis, makes a decision from the pool of choices. Such decisions fed into the minds of abusers for the attachment of a label that gives birth to the vexing pronouncement of being in recovery as a prerequisite for assistance. The so-called experts are at work remolding and categorizing the client and creating the client.

While trying to make sense of the assistance concept and the extension of help to those in need, extrapolations from current data were made. It was learnt that a majority of the client population, claiming in recovery, as they traversed several programs, have remained in recovery programs for a decade or more. The alcoholic experiences this process continuously throughout his life in rehabilitation programs. These approaches to providing help suggest that there is more to treating this population than we currently understand.

[23]According to the National Survey on Drug Use and Health, in 2011, an estimated 22.5 million Americans needed treatment for a problem related to alcohol or drugs- licit and illicit. Most of those seeking assistance rely on groups like Alcoholics Anonymous and Narcotics Anonymous, but only [24] "a fraction of alcoholics and addicts" make progress in such groups, according to Michael Fingerhood, head of Johns Hopkins University School of Medicine, a division of chemical dependency. To add insult to injury, according to a recent National Survey on Drug and Health, 60% of alcoholics and drug addicts relapse within one year. Yes, they are in recovery, as they themselves have defined, and using illicit substances and alcohol, while benefiting from assistance and free of responsibility.

How can this be, when would the alcoholic or drug addict be fully rehabilitated, and is this possible with psychotherapy? Or, should new approaches that integrate pharmaceuticals be considered, by building on an old consideration of Metabolic Adaptation and most recently, molecular reasons for addiction and subsequent dependency on alcohol or drugs?. We will talk about the latter question in a more detailed manner.

Dr. James R. Milan and Katherine Ketcham in their seminal work, Under the Influence, stated, "Physiology, not psychology, determines whether one drinker will become addicted to alcohol and another will not" and because of physiology, metabolic adaptation takes root in the liver primarily and secondarily in the brain where small amounts of alcohol is metabolized. Metabolic adaptation, therefore, creates a liver enzyme abnormality that becomes irreversible over time and subsequently prevents the alcoholic from eliminating acetaldehyde from the system. Metabolic Adaptation continues as alcohol is ingested. Remember the general biological rule, which holds that when a bodily system is under stress it either adapts or suffers damage. The body continues to adapt and to change to accommodate alcohol.

As stated earlier, a majority of my former clients detailed their struggles and inability to abstain from alcohol and illicit drugs while remaining in programs designed to assist them to maintain their stability. It would appear that efforts- counseling, aftercare, psychiatry, and mentoring programs- that were well intentioned became the mode used for perfunctory participation by most clients. It seemed like a vicious circle in acts of eternity. Clients continued doing what they had been doing because nothing seemed to trigger a response to cease their activities.

Something was going on within the sphere of the alcoholic and the drug addict that was incongruous within the framework of theory that was yet to gain credence. I attribute that missing component to nothing more than ongoing molecular changes. The latter can be described as rearranging the architecture and design of the addict's brain to function completely and respond in different ways to alcohol and drugs.

Permanent molecular and physiological changes have taken place in the addict and alcoholic. The first sign of change takes place in the liver and then the brain. In other words, since permanent changes have taken place, the addict and alcoholic react involuntarily to the demands created by metabolic adaptation. The alcoholic and drug addict is no longer in control and has no choice but to continue using both substances despite knowing the adverse effects. These involuntary indulgences- consuming alcohol and using illicit drugs- are the direct result of permanent changes in the brain and liver.

The struggle by the alcoholic and drug addict continues. He understands his dependency and addiction. He either makes a voluntary decision or coerced into seeking help. He quickly learns, while participating in alcohol or drug rehabilitation, that "relapse is part of recovery". The latter then becomes indelible in their language and being by leaving the window open for infrequent indulgences called relapse.

They have become trapped in a body without a soul.

GLORIA'S

Charles, an accomplished computer specialist with impeccable academic credentials from the number one school in the country and others, behaved like the English prince, hence the name. He started a relationship with alcohol at age 18 as a freshman. A few drinks on the weekend progressed to a daily drink or two. Over the years, Charles drank before breakfast, if any was prepared, while his girlfriend abused a legal drug- oxycontin- supposedly to alleviate pain in her legs, back, and arms.

Charles drank everyone under the table every Friday evening at Gloria's- a speakeasy- just to exclaim T.G.I.F (thank God it's Friday). This pronouncement of T.G.I.F was spontaneously made by the working public as a happy relief gesture; the weekend had arrived.

Gloria's was not a bar or restaurant or club neatly tucked away for the chosen few. The place had no signs outside to direct a patron where the action was taking place. You just knew about Gloria's if you were part of the drinking gentry.

Gloria's was located above two store fronts on a very busy commercial street. This street demanded good sight and driving skills all day long, as city buses jostle for driving space with cab drivers who were indifferent to everything but the next fare. The neighborhood was compared to living wild in the country.

On rainy days, this thoroughfare transforms itself into puddles of undetermined depths that hid potholes. Speeding cabs navigated around these hidden holes as they splashed water onto the sidewalk where patrons stood waiting for the local bus. Soaked commuters morphed into rude and obnoxious entities.

Cab drivers are a special kind; some are abrasive and annoying, while others are just oblivious to everything but the fare. I recall repeatedly instructing a driver to take the shortest route so that I would arrive on time for an important meeting, but the driver insisted that his way was faster. The ride was longer and consumed more time, yet the driver expected to be paid more than I was accustomed to paying. I refused and he became profane and threatening. As the only alternative, I reached into my jacket pocket to retrieve my phone to summon the local police. This action caused the driver to become jittery and he agreed to accept the fare that I was accustomed to paying.

It was common practice for cab drivers throughout large cities with many ethnic enclaves to stop abruptly in traffic for the next fare while remaining calm to the honking horns and obscene shouts from onlookers. To hear loud outbursts of Bomba Clot, a Jamaican profanity, as a reprimand, was part of the mix to challenge tolerance for the unknown.

I was advised that taking a cab ride to Gloria's would not be in my best interest. Walking would be the better option than being scared to death by unpredictable cab drivers known to demand additional payment to make a stop in front of Gloria's- PARKING PROHIBITED.

Gaining entry to the building and access to Gloria's was an exercise in ringing the bell three times, walking away from the door; remain standing aimlessly in the middle of the sidewalk, and waiting for an echo from two floors above. I performed this exercise with caution while looking around for the unknown. This kind of entry jujitsu is often used in such environments.

I was instructed to wait for a female voice to signal an acknowledgement of my presence. I waited for a few moments, and then I heard "Ooh dat?" There was no visual image to put life to the sound of the feminine voice. While pondering the next move, listening, hesitating, then responding with authenticity "Ah me."

When "Ah me" was said, the window opened but no one was seen. Within a few seconds, keys hastily thrown out the window. Gaining entry into the building was a challenge. Gaining access to the environment where patrons congregated was another challenge of tolerance.

After gaining entry into the building, trying to finding the apartment on the second floor seemed a mystery and a job for Sherlock Holmes. There were four doors on the floor without any sign designating an apartment number. The rule was to wait in the hallway until someone emerges from a door, and this could have been any door. The wait took an eternal 3 minutes.

Suddenly a male head emerged from a slightly opened door on the left. He looked left then right without any words uttered. The door closed, and then opened hastily.

"Got the keys?" the male asked. "Yeah" I responded. This was my first time going to Gloria's to meet an associate- Charles- who was already at the location. A long black hand signaled to me that it was time to enter and to discover the unknown.

At last I was at Gloria's and what a surprise. The venue turned out to be an apartment that was used as a bar, restaurant, and entertainment venue. I noticed an eclectic mix of patrons with all eyes looking at me with inquiry and suspicion. The loud chatter that I heard upon entering the apartment stopped and there was total silence. I was a newcomer.

Charles and G were seated on bar stools at the window facing the avenue. Both were looking periodically through the window as if in anticipation of a guest or just looking aimlessly outside for the unknown. "Have a drink, what do you want?" asked Charles in a rumbling manner slurring his speech.

Charles and I arranged to meet at Gloria's at 4pm, but Charles was there since 2pm. He wanted to get a head start with G who had been there since noon. To the right of Charles were two empty bottles of rum prominently displayed on a small dark center table that gave the appearance of time with clearly etched, yet old markings of drinking utensils. A few stained ashtrays on the table filled with brown cigarette butts and ends of rolled tobacco leaves that gave identity to Eddie's presence. It was drinking time.

"Get me another bottle of rum, and for my friend a beer." Charles signaled to an unknown person in the background. "Who is he?"

asked a female with an accent that implied an indistinguishable West Indian origin. Her voice had a sweetness of an undulating tenor playing a soothing tune to captivate the male senses. The accent was sweet to the ear and relaxing to the spirit.

A few voices in the background gave some distinct cultural identity, but it was challenging differentiating from where. There was a flavor of tantalizing mystery behind these voices. My ears were now sensitized in anticipation of another sound. I heard the next inquiry. It was a probing question with ambivalence. It inferred suspicion of the unknown. I became the unknown in every aspect. "I trust he is not the police, because you bring him without notice," the female continued with an irritating tone. "What's up with you woman, Just bring the liquor." stated Charles.

"You better get that one out of here. He is behind the curtain stretched out from too much daru. He has been here since early this morning. You know he was supposed to go to his program today, but who knows what good the programs are doing for him. He is still drinking like a fish. He is lucky that the City is still trying with him all these years. He got a warning last week. Boy that man can hold his sauce but he will lose his job cause of liquor". Such were the utterances from a short squatty black woman who emerged from behind the curtain.

Her smile was distinctive. A wide mouth accompanied a round face that overpowered by two sparkling gold incisors that complimented her snow-white teeth. It was a million dollar smile that brought warmth and gut feelings of comfort.

"O, here is the famous G, as in Gloria, the owner of this spot." stated Charles as he picked up the bottle of rum from the table and proceeded to open it. Charles was more focused as he gripped the bottle with both hands; kept his eyes on his twisting actions while motioning with his head in the direction where Gloria stood.

Gloria extended a handshake to me. She smiled with a tantalizing facial motion that had a very sexual overtone to accompany a body contoured as if Picasso had some input. Gloria was intensely charming and exhibited an air of entrepreneurial qualities as she mingling freely with everyone to assure that glasses were filled with spirits. You felt at home when Gloria made her presence known.

Charles raised himself up from the chair and wobbled. He held onto the nearby post adjacent to the hot water pipe for stability. The pipe gave Charles the support he needed to stand up, but not moving from that spot became a feat. He pointed in the direction of the curtain to draw attention to some kind of activity while mumbling something inaudible to everyone. Everyone had an inquiring look to decipher what Charles was saying.

"He's had enough, this is the third bottle between you two!" stated Gloria as she pointed directly at Charles and G. "You know I am responsible for everyone here in my apartment!" stated Gloria to Charles. "You an inspector or what?" asked G. "I ain't saying that but enough is enough," replied Gloria. "All five of you in here are going to alcohol programs, but for what? I don't get it," stated Gloria. "You know, if them people from the program see how we drink in the Caribbean and how all big man drink in the islands, everybody would be in programs. A few drinks don't hurt no body." came a resounding voice from the background, and from behind the curtain. It was Ted.

"Boy you awake. They have to do something with you people. Ted how long you been in this new program? Maybe a pill all ya all need because nothing is working for you all. Playing games with them people at New Compass or whatever is new about them. Maybe what is new is a needle or pill or something else. Wait until they catch you." stated Gloria.

"You are telling me how to drink liquor. Only in this country they talk about a few drinks like it's a big dealt." interjected another person. "Yea, I take care of business all the time, but they only keep talking about going into something for what they do." stated an onlooker from behind the makeshift bar. "Look man, I've been in all those recovery and alcohol programs but nothing works for me. Give me another drink before I leave." shouted another patron.

"This is what I do; drink when I don't have to go to the program. Always clean when they test the piss" remarked Charles. "But you can't do that forever." remarked Gloria. "So what do you want me to do? Look woman I have a family to take care of, and I'm doing what is necessary," continued Charles. "Big men, as you know, don't have to report to anybody," stated G.

"You are another one, see what the drinking did for you," stated Gloria as she looked with piercing eyes directly at G. "See how you get a big belly and leg problems; watch the veins on that right foot, them fat. When you going back to that doctor friend of yours, I bet he's scared to tell you what's up." Gloria stated bluntly.

"You talking Gloria, we all big people, I'll do what's good for me, everybody making a big deal about me and daru, so what," remarked Charles in a disgusting manner at Gloria's earlier statement. "So what's wrong taking a few drinks after works?" Charles mumbled aloud. "Yea" chimed in a few in the background in supporting Charles who kept on mumbling inaudibly yet directing his comments at Gloria. "All you here in this room, you put away the daru like water, take it easy." stated Gloria. "You getting to me Gloria, always talking about how much we drinking, we been doing this since in GT" interjected Charles. "Is time you ease up or stop drinking" stated Gloria.

"Like we've got to take our business elsewhere and very soon for everybody's health. What you want us to do or go Gloria, you making money here," stated Charles, in a somewhat condescending manner as he stared outside.

"Look, it is not that you shouldn't have a drink, but both of you are gone, and especially you G, first thing in the morning and last thing at night. Don't think I wasn't checking you out for a long time," Gloria stated in a very calm and reprimanding manner, as she looked at Charles and G directly into their eyes.

There was total silence in the room. The air in the room was already saturated with cigarette smoke that was thick enough to trigger a reflexive cough. There were a few coughs, not because of the dense and stifling smoke, but as a communication pause waiting for another voice to break the air of silence. Patrons started to shuffle reflexively.

All eyes moved from to right to left and back again. It seemed as if the eyes were challenging each other to make a responsive pronouncement. Ambivalence was the language that the physical bodies radiated. The silent bodies spoke and they understood each other and concurred to acquiesce to Gloria's fiery speech. It was not a speech, but a reprimand casted on all with the widest net. The statements made by Gloria left nothing in question that needed to be addressed but to be acted upon and now.

"Personally speaking, and I'll be honest, both of you need to check yourself out, I mean ask yourself if it good to drink liquor every day and all day without a break, your heart and liver, watch at you stomach man. Both of you always smell like liquor, is like you can't go nowhere without liquor" Gloria continued in a probing manner.

Then she became direct and personal. "Charles, you are always complaining about your stomach, but you don't eat, you don't even talk about nutrition. Moreover, that brings up the question and straight up talk now. All of you drinking too much daru. And you in particular, I smell you early in the morning when you are heading to work. Is daru the only thing you people want? How about some good pumpum on a weekend from a fresh cinting" Gloria asked as she stated her case while looking directly at Charles who kept a puzzled expression on his face.

Gloria was now treading on thin ice; talking about pumpum is stepping into the sexual zone. Gloria was questioning their virility and the sexual prowess they all claimed to have. Gloria was on fire, so she fired again, "Do you guys get any, or are you too drunk to do anything? From experience, those who drink like you all do, cannot get a hard on!" "It's a disappointment for a woman. Think about it, your woman wants some and you're always drunk." Gloria continued.

"She ain't talking about me," grunted a muffled voice. "What is this, a counseling sessions with that one downtown at you know where I am talking about?" asserted G, as he looked directly at Charles. "I go there and do what is needed," stated Charles. He was referring to the alcohol program he was attending by mandate. "Don't lie, you still drinking right here!" exclaimed Gloria. "You don't know it is not that I want to drink; something makes me drink. I know all the shit that those programs are about, and talk and more talk." Charles stated as he referred to his personal experience in alcohol rehabilitation during an inpatient stint.

"I ain't becoming a robot with the recovery shit at AA. Ain't got no problem, work, take care of business, do not commit crimes. Remember I did three programs. Same shit, just like the detox, and make little difference." stated Charles. "Look at you, can't even walk properly G, shaking and shit, can't stand up good" stated Gloria. "So what you want Gloria?" asked G.

"All I am saying is that too much liquor will create serious medical problems down the line. Ask yourself why you always have stomach problems Charles. It is the liquor. And you G, you better take care of them veins in your legs and your legs are flaky and swollen." advised Gloria.

"I'm afraid for you Charles. You cannot just stop drinking like that, and that is for you G too, you know. Both of you have to detox under medical supervision or else you gwine kill yourself. Remember Kass?" asked Gloria. "Yea, where is he, and the other one Lenny? I haven't seen them for a few months," stated Charles. "Somebody said that they both went to dry out at some hospital detox program" stated G.

"I heard that Kass, a real drinking man, is now behaving like a Christian and turning up his face at a shot of liquor. I heard that he met some doctor over there at the program, who referred him to another doctor that give him some kind of new medication and the man ain't drinking no more. That has to be some super shit and magic. The other one Lenny, a real hermit now, I heard that he can only drink so much now." continued G.

"Give me another drink and let me think about what I just heard, the two of them can't stop just like that. Some super shit or magic bullet or Jesus. This one got me!" commented Charles as he pondered what he heard. To his mind, and he was still convinced, that he can stop drinking when he wanted, but an inner voice kept whispering: Let's take a bet. His facial expression displayed an intensive and searching look that inferred an internal debate filled with questions.

"This is what I am going to do the next time I run into either Kass or Lenny; I'll ask about this new doctor and about the medication. Maybe I can get the referral numbers," advised Gloria.

"That sounds like a magic bullet. I heard someone speaking about some shit called gabapentin that he got at some research location in the city, but I don't know, that's something else!" stated Charles as he scratched his head in thought and contemplation.

Charles was last seen at his residence. It was not a pleasant sight. Before I made contact with Charles, I made a few telephone contacts with close friends who continued with unplanned visits with Charles. After all, he was experiencing a smaller world, as his needs were not beyond the boundaries of his established reservoir and fueling stations- All Saints Spirits and Johnny's Wings. Most were reserved in their true feeling, but reported that Charles had voluntarily confined himself to his apartment and was on the edge of reclusiveness while cohabitating with his paramour in a divided home. Both were living parallel lives of dependencies. It was also reported that Charles had refused to extricate himself from his home or to explore the changing environment around him.

His only contact with the outside world was by looking through the window to see cars and people bustling to their respective jobs early in the morning. To keep abreast of current events nationally and internationally, the choices became television, radio, telephone, and a quick trip to the corner store to purchase either cigarettes or milk and a momentary chatter with the grocery clerk. Charles stopped going to the supermarket, the laundry, or even buying clothing from the stores he frequented in times past. He had become a hermit and was trapped by his dependency on alcohol. He now shopped for alcohol by telephone and by associative means.

An old friend of Charles could not contain himself when describing what he thought of Charles. He restrained and seemingly was in a tussle with his brains and in desperation trying to use the most appropriate words for Charles. I saw from his fidgeting that there was a sense of apprehension as he delayed his words.

It was a difficult and arduous effort, and a task that added a sense of trying to deny the reality of what he had confronted on his last visit with Charles. He reached into his bag and extracted a cigarette. Strangely enough, he stared at the cigarette between his fingers as he slowly rolled it back and forth. He reached into his pocket and pulled out a Zippo lighter. He struck the lighter with his thumb and hesitantly adjusted the flame. He focused his eyes with a concentrated look on his face. He lit the cigarette and inhaled the fumes with a sense of contemplation and purpose. It seemed as if time stood still, as anticipation gripped my imagination. My listening skills were at work and I patiently waited for the silence to break.

This male an few years younger than Charles shook his head in a negative manner from left to right. He uttered unbelievable. His last visit with Charles was indeed unbelievable- Charles was accommodating and financing associates, who were less fortunate and dependent on alcohol, as he was, yet they all denied such a dependency. Because Charles was, now self- imprisoned and dependent on alcohol, a network of hangers-on, whose sole purpose was to drink, and to make it happen, as is said by the local and unemployable on a daily basis, became the new inhabitants of Charles' apartment. They were leaches!

Those new associates of Charles were busy at work early in the morning, and each day, making phone calls to him to begin their daily routine of drinking. Charles welcomed an early telephone call to alert him that the time was right to begin.

The oldest male in the group, who looked younger than the others did, always made the first call at 11:00am. This was followed by either one or two of the females who initiated the morning conversation by offering to go to the liquor store to make the purchase of their daily supply of spirits and beer. Charles was consistent with his request for cigarettes and rum. The women liked cheap vodka. The youngest males only settled for light rum while the older males only drank beer and volumes of it. Everything, and I mean alcoholic beverages, was paid for by Charles. He became The Federal Reserve Bank Chairman and similar to the Chancellor of the Exchequer, if the financing came from Britain.

Like most people, he knew that Charles received a large inheritance. He witnessed Charles spending sixty dollars on alcohol for the crowd. Not only was he funding the drinking frenzy, but he was also funding drugs used by a few of his newly acquired associates. Charles needed company for his indulgence, and was able to accommodate the hangers-on because he had the money to feed their addiction and dependency.

Abruptly he stopped talking and exclaimed, "It is a dam shame that such a good brother would fall prey to this type of shit!" I listened to this loosely made comment while contemplating my visit with Charles. I recalled that Charles made numerous commitments in general to visit close friends and associates in the community. He lived within walking distance of most of his friends yet he became a no show every time a promise was made.

A very close friend expressed to me two months preceding my visit, her concerns for Charles' medical and physical conditions. She exploded in a fit of anger as she talked about him while detailing her observations. She concluded that Charles could no longer socialize among persons who do not drink or even function in the absence of alcohol, as she observed when Charles attended an ceremony miles away from his residence.

Charles arrived at the celebration partially inebriated and became seemingly sober when he discovered that the function, because of religious reasons, did not serve alcohol. Charles abruptly left the venue and was reported to be at the local bar boosting his intake of alcohol, as another associate commented, before his resurgence drunk. It was embarrassing for her and the guests. Upon his return, his speech was slurred and his dialogue became repetitive with references to things in the past. His interaction with persons at the venue was looked upon sardonically.

I met Charles in his living room and he appeared disheveled. He needed a haircut, and a bath. He shuffled between the chairs in the living room, and walked with a limp as he held his right hip. His face showed lines of fatigue, and stress. His eyes were blood shot red with a black puffiness under the lids. At 3pm, he just got up from a long night's rest but was still very tired. He stumbled into the living room and positioned himself on the stained spot in the black leather sofa. Charles seated himself carefully but for some unknown reason he appeared to be seated in the same spot I left him a year earlier. The indented spot on the couch that was stained and outlined the markings of a body was his resting place. Not only was he sleeping there every night, but also he was conducting personal business with his associates in the same spot. Charles was grounded as a fixture to the sofa.

Parallel to the sofa was a large dusty wooden rectangular center table with a bric-a-brac collection of objects of unknown origin. He recalled being given those objects after his non-biological grandmother, with whom he spent most of his boyhood days, passed away in another continent, at age ninety nine. He pointed out with pride a few photographs of relatives, now collecting dust on the floor with other objects that were given to him by his deceased mother. On the wall were framed testimonials, awards, degrees, and old clippings from the local newspaper.

On the living room floor there was a collection of old newspapers from a year ago. The newspapers were stacked high and placed adjacently to the television of yesteryear. This collection he later pointed out to me, and commented, that it was important to have a hard copy for future reference. The burgundy colored rug was spotted with stain marks, cigarette burns, and looked black- it needed cleaning. Empty liquor bottles were displayed as trophies and adorned the area as symbols of indulgence. Underneath the entertainment center were two bottles of liquor tucked away as the emergency taste, as Charles referred to his stock.

As I engaged Charles, he rambled incoherently and repetitively talked about the same subject. Charles, at times, would not only repeat what he said five minutes ago, but had to be reminded that what he was referring to took place ages ago. He seemed to be stuck in a different place and time. Yet as we spoke, he referred to when things were different and of the good old days. Interesting enough, he questioned if those good old days were good ones to him.

As we spoke, I had to redirect Charles' conversation many times to gain a focus. It was like stepping on egg shells, in a gentle and informative manner, pointing out to him that the outer world was changing while he remained constant. Throughout our exchange, I teased him about his last venture into the contiguous neighborhoods six years ago. In general, I brought him current on how the community was progressively evolving with the infusion of a wide spectrum of talent and finance. He was surprised to hear that one of his best friends remained the owner of pristine property surrounded by developing real estate that seemed incongruous with the neighborhood.

He jostled with his memory to move his mind to think current, but was unable. He seemed stalled. As he listened, he would mechanically shake his head in approving anything that someone recollected; his short term memory was lost. He was lost in the present and firmly held on to the past as an anchor for his reference points in all conversations.

As we continued speaking, Charles took another drink then said, "I don't feel well, I feel a funny sensation in my head". He passed out and was immediately rushed to the emergency at a local hospital out of the community. This hospital was chosen because he always said that once he is coherent, while ill, to drive him over the bridge into the city. He made that choice because of their efficiency and promptness at seeing patients.

He was seen immediately and admitted to their intensive care unit. It was determined that Charles was suffering from an irregular heart beat and defined as a sinus arrhythmia; low potassium; lower blood pressure; chronic obstructive pulmonary disease; diabetes. Everything appeared to be wrong with Charles.

The attending physician bluntly stated that Charles' illness was directly attributed to his compulsive and excessively abusive consumption of alcohol, and smoking of too many cigarettes. He ended what seemed as a lecture by stating that Charles was "messed up" and needed alcohol rehabilitation, cessation of smoking, change of diet, and most of all, daily exercise. For some reason, he reacted with total disgust. He demanded immediate change from Charles.

Charles listened attentively and did not respond. He crimped his forehead, scratched his face, fidgeted with his wrist watch, and looked around his room as if he were looking for verbal ammunition to rebut the doctor. Charles got up with some effort and dropped back into the bed. There was not an utterance from him, but a blank stare of indifference to everyone present.

"That son of a bitch don't know anything about me, dam I'm in charge of me and I'll make the decisions on what to do! You know that I can stop drinking anytime I want, but smoking is a tough one," Charles stated to himself loudly, as all eyes became transfixed on him. The doctor returned to the room a few minutes later and addressed Charles directly. "You will be in alcohol detoxification beginning in the morning." "But I can stop drinking anytime I want doc." was his response.

"The years you have been drinking continuously has affected not only your heart, but your entire system. You see what has been happening to your legs with the swelling in the ankles and your distended stomach. We have to look more closely at the COPD tests to determine the best approach to treat your condition due to your lungs compromising on respirations." continued the physician.

"Oh, trying to stop on your own without medical supervision will be dangerous and not recommended, that's my position." He reprimanded Charles, with the authority of his position. "How many days do I spend in detox before I can go home?" Charles asked, with a sense of anticipating his discharge. "That's depends, and that can be up to 21 days, but there is more after the detox that has to be in place to help you to become well again. I believe that you want to enjoy those things you missed out on when you were very ill.," advised doctor. "What do you mean by more, doc?" Charles asked, with a rattling sound in his voice.

"Like aftercare, a smoking cessation coach, medication management, and things like that. There will be more details after your detoxification. Trust our skills you are in the right hands. Our will be seeing you for the next couple of days. Just rest and we'll make sure you are well cared for". "What does he mean by aftercare? We know he is not talking about some outpatient program to attend. Man, I had enough with the one I attended for eighteen months a few years ago when they snatched my license. I only had a few drinks. That tester was wrong, saying I had three times the legal limit. Whose limit and by what definition and from where did this all come from?" Charles asked with a sense of irritation.

Charles was doing all the talking. Everyone listened.

"Those group sessions- talking about the same old shit on a different day. All they talk about is avoiding complacency. All the telephone calls and those questionnaires are a bitch. All up in your business like spies. It is like kindergarten classes. My family has nothing to do with my situation. I'll handle my shit!" Charles continued. "Baby we all love you and want for you to do well. We are all here to support you in this challenge. We know it's not going to be easy, but we are here with you." A voice assured him.

Charles just sat on the bed with his head lowered. He stared at the floor with piercing eyes as he moved his head from left to right. He seemed to be tracking an unknown object as he continued moving his head. From time to time, he would stop and look intensely at one area on the floor then crinkled his forehead as his eyes focused. These actions inferred that a deep thought process was taking place. The comments being voiced were nothing new to Charles- he had heard them many times before from his primary physician and family members.

Ten days later Charles was reported to have signed himself out of the hospital and returned to his residence. I was not surprised, but concerned and fearful of the long term ramifications by his actions.

A few telephone calls to old associates, who worked at the institution, to get some germane information on Charles prior to his involuntary discharge was necessary. But I was not successful in gaining a realistic profile of Charles. So I decided to call him at his residence.

"Charles how you doing?" was my opening question when he answered his phone. "Great I was discharged a few days ago, things are looking up.", Charles responded. His voice was clear with an air of freshness. He sounded cognitively attuned and did not ramble in any manner, as he had done on prior occasions while ingesting volumes of alcohol. It was a good feeling to hear Charles cogently responding with a sense that he accomplished a mission.

"How's the family doing, and the lady?" I inquired. "Look, stop by when you get a chance or if you are free now, come on over" Charles stated. I went over to Charles a few hours later. He answered the door and motioned me into the apartment. He had a warm and cheerful fixed smile on his face. The apartment smelt fresh and free of the residual effects of second hand smoke. The living room was surprisingly clean and free of old newspapers or empty liquor bottles. Dust now seemed a foreign element on the center table that had been hidden of its choice wood from years of air borne deposits. The twenty year old giant monstrosity of a fifty four inch television, which distorted images with poor quality color, was replaced by a forty two inch flat screen. There were signs of change.

We exchanged pleasantries and chatted for a while. His paramour spoke of some of the changes made in the home while Charles was in detox. Because she suffered from numerous ailments, and pains throughout her body, help from a neighbor to clean and to dump whatever needed to be out of the home, became expensive.

According to her, the most recent crisis in Charles' life had to be the wakeup call for his journey towards sobriety. However, over the last couple of days, he was reverting to the very substance that caused him to be hospitalized and is the direct contributor to all his ailments and, in particular, his heart and stomach problems. Without question, her tolerance for this repetitive behavior became exhaustive.

As Charles spoke, he kept a vigil on his watch. He just could not help himself, but to keep looking at the time. He seemed to be going somewhere or waiting for a specific time to do something. Abruptly in the middle of our conversation, Charles stood up and stated, "I can have one now."

Charles was back on the bottle! He drank more than before, and daily. His kidneys and liver stopped functioning. He succumbed to both diseases.

HERE DO WE GO FROM HERE?

We always hear persons from the caring professions referencing valid reasons, causes, effects, and contributory factors to unravel the mystery of addiction and dependency.

Explanations are always given but everything within the explanations becomes a variable. The components of the variables go from environmental, cultural, social, educational, and even economic factors. All these have been linked to illicit substance use and abuse. All of these contributing factors add clarity in the ongoing discussions of alcoholism and dependency. These factors only add more to the explanations of cause and effect.

However, very little attention is placed on the addict and alcoholic that is predisposed to abusing substances because of an addictive personality. Numerous studies have stated that there are a number of physiological differences between alcoholics and non-alcoholics. In the alcoholic metabolic adaptation coupled with molecular changes predisposes them to the vulnerability of alcohol.

It has also been suggested in some studies that bipolar disorder, attention deficit disorder, and chronic depression predisposes all individuals to addiction and dependency. Some other studies have stated that the dependencies follow the illness quite often. Interestingly enough these disorders all have a physiological link when carefully studied, yet the thrust of intervention implies the psychological approach to treatment.

However, it appears that every discussion on addiction and dependency, despite the inclusion of physiological factors, remain contingent on the "if" and "it depends" and "possibility" and "probability", as most so-called experts would say, to give an explanation that is linked to the psychological, yet not an answer. Therefore, according to this thinking, the root of the addiction and dependency then becomes a psychological one. As such, issues of addiction or dependency become psychological.

It seems that prefixing the explanation of alcoholism and drug addiction only leaves the recipient of the information hanging in anticipation for an answer. The prefixing of all discussions appears to lay the pathway for a predetermined conclusion, when germane questions are asked about addiction and dependency that points in another direction.

Explanations often lead to more explanations buried in psychological evaluations, psycho socials, psychiatric evaluations, case assessments, family evaluations, and agency conferences. Reports from these sources add to documentation whereby more time is spent recording known and effluent information that paves the way for the CYA (cover your ass) syndrome that is rampant in all bureaucracies. The blending and sharing of information throughout this web of connectivity with every specialist in their respective field adds more quantitative understanding, but gives less qualitatively meaning to the uplifting of the addict and alcoholic free of his misery.

It becomes academic exercises. The addict and alcoholic remain with the misery of their existence. It becomes even more complicated when a bureaucracy, which employs experts in every discipline, is called to exercise judgment to fulfill a mandate to provide protection to families and children who are the victims of alcohol and drug addicted caregivers. These experts are adherents to what is now called by academics and researchers "cosmetic psychiatry" that is filled with ambiguities, yet they are given the authority, by licensing, a mandate to provide information for judicial action. The experts are thus locked into reiterations of the same information to corroborate what had already been established.

To understand this vicious confluence of information sharing, the bureaucracy is always called upon to render judgment on written reiterations to meet their mandate for funding. Because of funding, the unavoidable review of records activities intertwined with explanations, reports, and recommendations, which were all by-products of reviews. It became a game whereby everyone covered his turf. It was simply documentation on an ongoing basis.

Purveyors of the art and professionals of intervention services are caught in the zone of "Unspecified Mental Disorders", as detailed in the DSM-5 (see pages 66, 122, 708). As page 708 clearly and unapologetically stated that the new application of the title UMD, must be made for those who "do not meet the full criteria for any mental disorder". More activities and more recommendations and more reviews. It became an unending set of tasks to satisfy mandates with lots of paper trails.

CYA (cover your ass) is real and always appeared active. The pressure was on then and still is on again.

Explanations, always with an emphasis on the psychological and with psychiatric overtones, seemed to be the norm. The quick fix became the answer with medications and intervention to assist in alleviating the stressful effects of dependency. This was how it was in the real world order of the helping professions. It became a vicious circle filled with explanations propelled by mandates. There were always memos and new directives following a situation that truncates or disrupts a procedure.

Yet explanations of addiction and dependency, engulfed and supported by theory, still did not provide enough insight to give weight for the core problems of addiction and dependency. This is not to deny the importance of psychological factors used to explain associative behaviors of dependency, but there was something not understood.

[24]Dr. Nora Volkow, director of the National Institute on Drug Abuse, stated, "successfully treating addiction will require a combination of behavioral and cognitive counseling with prescription of multiple medicines tailored to the phase of recovery and targeting both the light and dark side of dependence". The National Institute on Drug Abuse is now supportive, because of new research, that efforts to rehabilitate must not be solely focused on the psychological. Rather, a combination of psychological and

largely the physiological factors need more focus. What a shift in thinking!

Despite recognition by Dr. Volkow that the current approaches that has, as its focus, the psychological, needs to integrate with other efforts in addressing problems of addiction, she went further by stating that more is "needed in the understanding of addiction."

The missing connection still needed to be explored.

FIGHTING THE DEMONS

[26]Mike Tyson, former boxing heavyweight champion of the world, was trained and disciplined every moment of his professional life while under the dictates of his personal trainer Cus D'Amato. Tyson boasted of discipline and its effects on his functioning in the boxing arena. Discipline paved the way and made the difference for him to become the champion. However, when questioned about his disciplined ability vis-à-vis addiction, he responded, "discipline isn't that something to strive for each New Year; it's necessary for every moment" and admitted "it was not enough to stop my side of addiction". He recognized the importance of discipline, and was able to understand its minimal role in keeping him at bay from his urges and indulgences, which brought about by addiction and dependency.

Mike Tyson had been receiving psychological intervention for years. Therapy influenced him to recognize the need to explore reasons beyond his disciplined self and his psychological complexities for his continued failings to maintain sobriety. As the fight with the demons of his addiction continued, he was beginning to make mental notations that there was something else missing in his life. He understood that it was not discipline nor a lack of an in depth understanding of what propelled him to indulge in behaviors against his desires. Rather, it was what he called, the "something else" that he was yet to understand. He also knew, understood, and recognized that his negative behaviors had consequences, yet he continued with his indulgences.

Think about the concept of discipline for a moment by reflecting on your own success that emanated from discipline in academics or sports. Now juxtapose your discipline, while struggling to end an indulgence of either drugs or alcohol that had the ether in your functioning for over a decade or longer. An internal fight begins, then you recognize that discipline becomes impotent and secondary to the commands of addiction and dependency.

It is common knowledge within the helping profession that alcohol and drugs win every time. They overpower and subjugate discipline to an infantile state of helplessness. Either one becomes king and master and controller of the total person to the point of enslavement. Yet, the power of the devil in a bottle, as some functional alcoholics describe their world of dependency, is treated solely as rooted in psychological issues, while an understanding of the permanent changes within them fails to gain attention, focus, and recognition. The concept of irreversible change that ignites the propensity to continue with drug habits must be at the forefront.

There are two main reasons why alcohol and drug habits are difficult to break. Let us look.

1. Alcohol and drugs make changes that, transform the brains chemical architecture to function and respond differently when not fed by alcohol. The transformation is permanent.

2. Alcohol and drugs are chemicals.

The brain's chemistry is altered and changed by the introduction of and subsequent abuse of alcohol or drugs. The chemical changes are irreversible in the brain. Because of this permanency, the brain no longer can tolerate anxiety or tension. Once the brain loses its natural ability to tolerate normal stress and anxiety that is tolerated by the average person, the physiology is out of balance. The mild disruptions caused by environmental stress and anxiety cannot be ameliorated or managed by nature's own mechanisms to maintain functionality. Therefore, the balancing agent is either alcohol or drugs.

In the alcoholic, it is clearly seen that alcohol becomes, so to speak, the therapy, that is needed to maintain equilibrium. Tension or anxiety can only be eased with more ingestion of alcohol and nothing else. This is so because alcohol consumption laid the groundwork for the changing of the chemistry in the brain, and the change is PERMANENT. Like it or not the alcoholic is incapable of reversing the changes in the brain chemistry.

Tyson, in his memoir Undisputed Truth, described himself as an addict after his retirement from boxing in 1986. Because of his acceptance of the title- addict-, he was able to begin his walk to sobriety, according to the memoir, but permanently refraining from alcohol indulgence became elusive. Tyson's walk to sobriety only focused on his psychological trappings as the basis for his addiction, but failed to give any credence to the changed factors. He continued receiving psychotherapy, which enabled him to maintain some semblance of stability.

Yet, he continued to abuse substances, and recognized that his behaviors were incongruous and beyond his control. He just did, not what his intellect told him, but succumbed to the body's demands for the chemicals (alcohol and drugs) that led to the permanent changes in his brain's chemistry. Tyson remained, as he described, "helpless" to alcohol.

Here is the problem.

We now know that once there are changes in the brain's chemistry, it is PERMANENT. Yet, practitioners within the helping profession remain steadfast with their heads buried in the sand by seeing the issues of alcoholism and drug addiction as a psychological one, and not rooted in the physiological changes that requires chemistry as the intervening agent for balance. Alcohol and drugs are the chemicals needed for this balance. The profession seems to believe that chemical changes can be reversed by intensive psychotherapy, although evidence abounds that the latter does help in addressing the pathology, but not a solution for addiction.

A failure by professionals to go beyond what they have been taught, learned, and observed, immediately puts an end to their mission towards sobriety for clients who are seeking meaningful help with their addiction. Professionals, who continue to inculcate in sessions with clients that addiction rests on the psychological, creates a new crutch for the addict. This approach gives power to the addict and alcoholic, in an unintended way, to accept the status of what I term psychologically addicted permanence. This then becomes the precursor for the inculcation of phrases like, recovering addict and recovering alcoholic, to reinforce the newly minted label that the alcoholic and addict attaches to defining himself or herself.

Just the acceptance of the addict label and by extension the absence of the word permanent, a voice and power is given to the phrase in recovery, as used by participants of structured programs of rehabilitation. In recovery is now used synonymously with the ongoing process of recovering which is ongoing, and in anticipation of attaining a substance free existence. It does not suggest putting an end to old activities.

In recovery takes on a new meaning that accommodates and compliments the human instincts of urges, wants, and ultimately, needs. It also implies a purification of the self towards change, while allowing free choice to open the gates for continued indulgence. The addict and alcoholic are now on their journey of perpetuity within programs, without an end in sight!

By exercising freewill that voluntarily accepts the ingrained rote phrase- in recovery-, it empowers the alcoholic and drug abuser to test discipline. But discipline is not enough, because utterances of in recovery have become the vehicle that clears the path to justify and accept that relapse is a part of recovery. It is an anticipation of a relapse that the addict or alcoholic expects to occur during the process towards sobriety.

Relapse is seen as part of the substance abuse disorder, and having its genesis in psychological problems, and as such, is treated in that manner. Relapse is also taught and seen as interruptions in the process leading to the "recovering alcoholic" concept. One cannot be in recovery and experience relapses at intervals, and on a continuous basis, while anticipating sobriety hence, despite recognizing the internal propensity to consume. It is beyond dependency.

The reasons are molecular.

Once again, Tyson vowed to get sober after the accidental death of his 4 year daughter Exodus in 2009. He remained substance free for about five years. During those five years, the urge to dabble socially taunted Tyson in a challenging manner to which he ultimately surrendered.

During August 2013, Tyson, once again, relapsed and returned to the concurrent theme of "recovering alcoholic". This time there was a twist that reinforced the theme when he stated, "recovery is a drawn -out process" while incorporating into his language the known and accepted phrase, "relapse is a part of recovery". He was hooked on the concept of recovery, not recovered.

Tyson, like the majority of people in rehabilitation programs, have succumbed to rote learning: a process of memorization through repetition without understanding and without any independent thought. Relapse, as part of recovery, is acceptable but not encouraged, because it is part of the process to sobriety. He was like a parrot imitating what was said.

Despite adhering to this dictum, Tyson stated that, "it is extremely difficult to develop a sober and moral consciousness without a good support system" in the struggled for sobriety. Here I agree with Tyson who emphasized the word good, and not just a supportive system of people, whose presence are symbolic as damage control measures for a crisis. Rather, the support must be continuous in a network of methods- friends, family, collaterals, religious institutions, and organizations that provide a new environment for association.

It is very important to recognize the need for a good support system as the camaraderie that shields the abuser from self - infliction of relapse. The latter occurs when an internal sense challenges the self to have a momentary indulgence. Such challenges are powerful especially during periods when celebration of an event is significant, such as, the birth of child or a daughter or son graduating from college.

Many former clients detailed their experience from relapse infliction. Many stated that their spontaneous response to having a drink at celebratory events propelled them to begin the process of incremental indulgences. Progressive indulgences became the link to relapse infliction, and such actions, contributed to the ongoing involvement in recovery programs into infinity. It was an ongoing process of seeking out programs for salvation from their own indulgences. All agreed that their support systems were weak because it did not act as the repellent that wards off and aligns the impulse of indulgence to refrain from old behaviors. Programs became the crux of their existence.

While long term recovery remains the goal and top priority of clinical interventions, it must be truncated and replaced by the phrase I refer to as: recovered with support. The later provides the new mantra for the abuser to see freedom from the continuum coat of recovering, and the involvement with programs. Such an approach gives the abuser hope that recovery can happen and is attainable. A good support system facilitates and gives life and meaning to the status of recovered. The alcoholic therefore gets a new understanding of the word recovered, which now connotes a better accounting of the present state of the former abuser.

It would appear that interventions have had far less effect in helping substance abusers maintain changes for long term recovery. It appears that only when an abuser accepts the reality of his body's assimilation to accommodate alcohol abuse, functional stability then becomes the goal. Just the acceptance of this understanding brings about a new reality that allows the abuser to understand that the physiological changes, brought about chemically, are permanent, and as such, need a different approach to keeping them functionally stable.

Programs, which continue to emphasize defined stages of recovery, as the building blocks that would eventually lead to the goal of sobriety, are making a one size, fits all prescription for all abusers. Some abusers were suffering from psychological problems and all abusers have been the by-product of permanent chemical changes.

It must also be recognized that each person is different in every sense- genetically and physically. A failure to recognize that humans are different and that their needs are different will always result in one standard approach to address the needs of the abuser. Such an approach by clinicians will continue to extend the abusers participation in rehabilitation programs into INFINITY! We must move beyond such thinking.

ASSUMPTIONS OF RECOVERY

Recovery assumes a continuum over time, whereby the approach to recovery takes on, the so-called systematically or the one-day at a time change in behavior. These small but incremental changes in behaviors have a direct correlation with mental changes. Recovery, as in a mental health thought processes, has numerous influences on the behavior that is manifested. And those mental changes that influence new behaviors will contribute to health and personal growth. It further assumes that emotional healing is the key that unlocks the door to a new functioning of the alcoholic and drug addict. The focus then becomes emotional healing to bring about change.

Relapse assumes a reversion to a previous state of dysfunction according to (Annis & Davis, 1989; Groski, 1986). In other words, it is going back to what you were doing at an earlier time. Relapse then is not a singular event, but an incremental process that predicts a future event and, is taught as such. Relapse spells out an always present time bomb that can be ignited by the alcoholic and drug addict, through their behaviors of indulgences. Indulgences, therefore, become the fuel that ignites and causes the battle between the alcoholic and him or herself to remain in the present.

We have seen that terms and active words like recovery and recovering are deeply rooted only in the psychological state of the alcoholic or drug addict, because the actions of this population are the precursors on the road to establishing and demonstrating that recovered is tainted and an ongoing process. Recovered seems to have been excluded from the lexicon, while recovery, the process, is the appendage to the continuum of recovering. The process never ends at recovering. Stagnation of growth will be the result. The process, therefore, becomes a continuous and never changing task that traps and renders immobile all efforts by the alcoholic and addict to make changes.

The focus of treatment, at most rehabilitation centers, becomes the psychological and by extension and assumption, behavioral changes will result. However, when permanent physiological changes, as we have discussed, are brought about by chemical changes in the brain, caused by alcohol or drugs, a specific need is created by a specific agent. In the alcoholic the agent becomes alcohol and in the case of the drug addict the agent becomes drugs. As was stated earlier, relapse has taken on a meaning that empowers the abuser because he or she subscribes to the taught message that relapse is part of the healing process. Relapse gives comfort to the abuser that redemption can be sought and granted within the circle of rehabilitation providers. Relapse as if detoxification has become the game to access needs and wants.

Most alcoholics have confessed to voluntarily submitting to in-patient assignment whenever they believed that there was a need to free the body of drugs. Some addicts and alcoholics see this approach as a break in their indulgence. Detoxification helps in the short term. However, most alcoholics and addicts admitted to only doing the stabilization phase of rehabilitation and were not committed to completing the process- they wanted something that was quick.

Those who attended rehabilitation programs for years felt frustrated with agencies that had large turnover in staffing. These clients believed that there were too many changing faces to identify with, as the real helpers. Clients felt as if they were a deck of cards being shuffled and dealt out to whoever was present to provide intervention. Most did not feel the client- therapist relationship as bonding for a specific goal. As such, engagements with therapist, according to many, became perfunctory. For many clients, intervention was always, as many stated "information gathering" by new staff members and new clinicians.

Most felt that reiterating known and established information to caseworkers, counselors, and psychiatrists was a tedious exercise in regurgitating information already contained in their history file. Many stated that clinicians were overworked, lazy, or preoccupied with other issues that were very demanding and took priority.

It appeared that the only focus of abusers was detoxifying the body of drugs while deferring engagement in the other phases of treatment. They chose to free their system of drugs or alcohol under supervised conditions because they recognized that detoxification can be life threatening, and requires medical management due to withdrawal stress during the first seventy- two hours. Remember, clients were not stupid but indulged in stupid behaviors, which they recognized, and as such, beyond their control.

It seemed that the actions of abusers were counterproductive after they completed detoxification then reverting to past behaviors. Most of those who indulged in this voluntary detoxification, and on a regular basis, stated that they remained trapped by an impulse and compulsion to start indulging in their substance of choice. Every client agreed that counseling sessions, while informative and understood by them, failed to act as a deterrent from established behaviors.

Although clients were counseled that treatment of substance abuse disorder was an ongoing process, and that it was segmented into stages of recovery that can be protracted into years, most felt a need to speed up the process. They wanted something more meaningful that leads to sobriety, and not just psychological stability, but total freedom from substances. The participants wanted an answer that was quick.

But being trapped in the psychological state of recovery which excludes all consideration of factors rooted in the physiological state of the alcoholic, creates a problem. When there is a failure to recognize that the physiological state, once changed chemically, there is no reconstructing, and in this case the brain's architecture, and to do what biology designed it to do in controlling anxieties or stress which are beyond the abilities of the addict or alcoholic.

Alcoholism is not a disease, as is defined and generally accepted in clinical practices, but an irritant chemical that does permanent transformation that demands the abuser's needs to be fed with alcohol as the fuel; thus making the reality of dependency without surety of a cure. Since there is no cure for the alcoholic to be found in the counseling approach beyond attempts to strive for stability and meaning in the alcoholic's life, it is rational to assume that something is yet to be unearthed.

We also know that there is no known cure for substance use disorder. Hence, prevention remains an ongoing process to keep in check the high probability of relapse becoming a reality without alternatives. And, the latter, remains a repetition of what is already known by the abuser, through numerous encounters while at in-patient rehabilitation programs. The cycle of programs continues for the alcoholic.

Abusers have stated that their ongoing involvement with rehabilitation programs have become tedious exercises in acquiescing to authority to which they are ultimately accountable. Most of them have expressed a desire to be freed of programs because they have recognized that a cure for their alcoholism is not a reality. However, most wanted an Antidote.

THE ANSWER

On December 24, 2013, the subject of metabolic adaptation in the liver was explored and it was conclusively linked to molecular changes in the brain, which lays the foundation for alcoholism. Primarily, molecular reasons were given serious thought on the issues of addiction and dependency, while metabolic adaptation was seen as laying the foundation and path for the latter. This was very refreshing.

These findings, recently published in a JAMA (Journal of American Medical Association) study, led by Dr. Mason, added the explanation to a difficult question. It answered why alcohol and drug habits are so difficult to break. The findings also pointed the way to new medicines to help addicts go cold turkey. It was a complete deviation from what is currently known about alcohol and drug effects on the brain.

A brief review:

The known: The heavy use of alcohol and drugs work on reward centers in the brain to drive addiction and dependency.

New Research Findings, published November 2013, in JAMA Internal Medicine and early testing at the National Institute on Alcohol Abuse and Alcoholism stated the following:

[24] "Alcohol's impact on the brain transforms its chemical architecture bringing about change (molecular change). Drinking and drug use triggers feelings of anxiety and tension that can only be eased by more consumption." In other words, structural changes become irreversible and permanent because of alcohol and drug abuses.

According to the new findings, attempts to treat only the emotional issues are a problem in itself. The study also pointed out that progress becomes impeded by not treating the physiological component. Interestingly enough, the study emphasized that the psychological as well as the physiological issues must be addressed simultaneously in order to achieve any progress. It is attacking the problem on two fronts.

Therefore, the thrust of treatment for the abusers must begin with accepting that the main problem is physiological. If not, psychological intervention would render the purpose of rehabilitation impotent because the unknown physiological changes have never been considered, or treated. Without the recognition that the main culprit is the physiological, all attempts at intervention will become an exasperating exercise filled with hopeless and redundant efforts.

Because treatment is primarily focused on psychological issues as primary factors contributing directly to abuse of substances, progress towards sobriety becomes a pipe dream for the alcoholic and drug abuser who wants to stop but knows that something internally, not psychologically, propels their indulgences. Clinicians recognize there is more to the abuse issue beyond the psychological, yet only treat one.

Despite this continued approach, there are a miniscule number of medical practitioners engaged in addiction research studies, who are now recognizing and giving credence to the physiological impact on the alcoholic. It is the permanency and irreversible aspects they have finally seen. At the same time, those who are currently treating the psychological issues of the alcoholic, and not trained to recognize the physiological issues that have become permanent in the alcoholic, are swimming against the tide of progress.

It is the recognition of the ongoing metabolic adaptation in the liver and the molecular changes in the brain, which becomes permanent, that need to be addressed. If not addressed, abusers will continue to seek relief from addiction and dependency while the stressful effects of dependency are left untreated. Thus, treating the stressful effects of alcoholism cannot be addressed in any other way but by pharmaceutical intervention.

This myopic focus on the psychological by many clinicians, coupled with their failure to give consideration or make an association with metabolic adaptation and molecular changes as the major factors contributing to alcoholism, and molecular changes for drug addiction, contributes to the minimal progress made by this population in rehabilitation programs. The abusers remain grounded in futile attempts at rehabilitation, while engaged in already known therapies, and not moving towards sobriety.

The good and positive news is that a connection has been finally made between metabolic adaptation and molecular reasons in understanding the alcoholics' struggle to be freed from the chains of dependency. The connection gives new hope to the abusers of alcohol and drugs, who knew that something was impeding their progress, but were unable to identify the true culprit.

The focus of intervention must be one of moving the substance abusers from the protracted withdrawal syndrome, which manifests itself in irritability, anxiousness, and mild depression. The abuser understands himself or herself in a personal way, yet, once involved in rehabilitation, involuntarily becomes inculcated and acclimated to prattles: I'm in recovery or I am a recovering ------, to define his or her existence. The abuser needs to move beyond the trap of in recovery to a new plateau defined by functional with parameters.

Those substance abusers that I interviewed initially defended the two phrases as meaningful to define themselves after ongoing engagements in rehabilitation. Yet, it was more an acceptance of their status as functional alcoholics or drug addicts who had made the conscious decision to indulge within given parameters. Others felt that they had inculcated the phrases to remain relevant within the continuum of their personal journey towards being substance free. Most felt that they had recovered to the point of being only social drinkers.

MYTHS

A mere digression is needed here in order to get a clear connection between metabolic adaptations in the liver and molecular changes in the brain. Before we spell out the connection between the two, let us look at a few more MYTHS and REALITIES of alcoholism, as detailed in Under the Influence by Dr. James R. Milam and Katherine Ketcham, which stated as follows:

MYTH: Alcohol is an addictive drug, and anyone who drinks long and hard enough will become addicted.

REALITY: Alcohol is a selectively addictive drug; it is addictive for only a minority of people.

MYTH: Addiction to alcohol is psychological.

REALITY: Addiction to alcohol is primarily physiological. Alcoholics become addicted because their bodies are physiologically incapable of processing alcohol normally.

MYTH: People become alcoholics, because they have psychological or emotional problems, which they try to relieve by drinking.

REALITY: Alcoholics have the same psychological and emotional problems as everyone else before they initially started drinking alcohol.

According to Ketcham and Milam, these problems are aggravated by their addiction to alcohol, as exemplified by the alcoholic's inability to cope with the everyday problems of living. It is a fact that alcohol has deleterious effects on the brain that causes severe physiological changes that contributes to emotional distortions of the normal personality.

The early symptoms of alcoholism are clearly visual to anyone who has observed the drinker's propensity to consume a few more drinks, every time, than was consumed on any prior occasion. It is the persistency of the pattern of drinking. There seems to be no variation to the pattern of drinking. It becomes the "one drink more syndrome".

One would also notice the increased consumption appears to have no further effect on the alcoholic. Actually what we see is the body's ability to adapt to the increased alcohol intake. It is this adaptation, by the liver, as well as other organs, which begin physical dependence.

Let us look at how this works.

As alcohol becomes routinely ingested, the body, as a system, goes through changes to accommodate alcohol. The cells in the body slowly and progressively begin to adapt by making changes in their structure. These changes are particularly evident in the liver and the central nervous system. The process of ongoing changes continues while consumption drives and speeds up the process of adaptation that leads to permanent changes.

As incremental cellular structural changes begin to take place, the body is at work on two fronts- physiologically and structurally- to arrive at efficiency of function and tolerance. In other words, the changes made on the two fronts are similar to converting a system from one fuel source to another for efficiency and functioning. In the body, it becomes total adaptation of the liver while progressive structural changes in the brain continue.

Continued abuse of alcohol places body's system under assault. This constant assault forces the body to either adapt or die. The body adapts, as any organism would, in line with the need to survive. However, the adaptation is to an insidious and continuous battle, while the process of incremental damage begins and continues. The damage is slow, silent, and continuous. At the same time, the by -product of alcohol, acetaldehyde, seeping from the liver, begins its journey of destruction of the brain. Molecular changes (chemical) have arrived with long lasting health repercussions.

It is interesting to note that it is an acceptable myth that measures can be taken to alleviate the reaction by the body, as a system, to alcohol ingestion, by using various methods. Heavy drinkers, like social drinkers, subscribe to the notion that a good meal preceding the intake of alcohol takes care of business, and the business here is to maintain a sense of equilibrium and cognition. It is true that a good meal only helps in slowing down the absorption and diffusion processes. Others believe that ingesting a portion of olive oil, "coats the stomach" to slow down absorption of alcohol. The extreme of drinkers, on the other hand, would consume volumes of alcohol then regurgitate as a form of rehabilitating the stomach.

The alcoholic and social drinkers are yet to recognize that 95% of alcohol consumed is metabolized in the liver, while only 5 % is diffused by excretion and evaporation- breath, urine, sweat, feces and saliva. The liver and kidneys are primary filters, but unlike oil and transmission filters in a car, it cannot be replaced, and are under assault to do the job of removing the toxic by -products of alcohol. Drinking alcohol everyday only keeps the purification systems of the body working in overdrive. A distended stomach attests to the effects of excessive drinking in most alcoholics.

In 2011, according to the [23]National Survey on Drug Use and Health, more than 21 million American needed treatments for problems related to alcohol and drugs, but a greater amount needed intervention for alcohol abuse. As of 2013, the number of substance abusers seeking treatment rose to 23 million and escalating.

Stunningly, it has been reported that only a fraction of alcoholics and drug addicts who seek treatment from support groups like Alcoholics Anonymous and Narcotics Anonymous show any improvement in their status, while the majority relapse within one year of trying to kick the habit. According to the federal government's National Survey on Drug Use and Health, 60% of alcoholic and drug addicts who seek help, and are in treatment, and do relapse in the first year. From these findings, we can infer that there seems to be an unknown entity that triggers the urge to use and subsequently abuse alcohol or drugs that we are yet to understand.

[24] Michael Fingerhood, who heads Johns Hopkins University School of Medicine, division of chemical dependency, confirms that support groups like those that AA and NA, only work, "in a fraction of alcoholics and addicts". Here is an admission that AA and NA programs cannot work to the extent of removing the urge to use. It appears that these programs are designed with the liberal "keeping at bay" approaches, and as such, they remain relevant but not successful in motivating the abuser to stop or to be moderate. Something is still lacking that needs to be investigated.

Research, published in November 2013 in JAMA Internal Medicine, stated that, "the brain's stress response also contributes to dependence and is the primary factor that plays "a direct role" in addiction. Here we see that the thinking is beginning to move in the direction of physiology to give the explanation to the mystery of addiction. It is also the recognition that the static approaches currently being used to treat alcoholics and drug addicts are only tools that keep in check, as I refer to the efforts, the propensity to consume excessively.

This acceptance by JAMA of the direct role that physiological changes play, and its contribution leading up to dependency, opens the doors for a new focus. The acceptance and ambivalent receptiveness of additional contributors to alcoholism, therefore, dictates that treatment for alcoholics and drug addicts, whose dependency is rooted in physiology, needs to look for another approach that is rooted in pharmacology. We cannot remain myopic to the recognition that the most promising approach places greater emphasis on the physiological and not on psychological.

[24]Dr. George Koob, director of National Institute on Alcohol Abuse and Alcoholism, who pioneered the study on the dark side of addiction, by moving the discussion from the psychological to

the physiological, stated that the years of heavy drinking or drug use causes the, "remodeling of the circuitry in and around a part of the brain known as the Amygdala where feelings of anxiety are triggered". The process of addiction has now moved through assimilation in the liver and leads to permanence by transforming the brain's chemical architecture; this cannot be reverted to its original state.

Dr. Koob stated that the brain's Stress Response System around the Amygdala goes into a state of permanent "overdrive" and yearning for fulfillment when alcohol or drugs are absent. The presence of alcohol or drugs prevents the Amygdala from going into the overdrive mode. The presence of alcohol or drugs represents the balancing ingredient for maintaining equilibrium of the brain and liver.

The Journal of Clinical Investigation concurs with this description and stated, "The Amygdala is believed to play a key role in assigning significance to specific sensory input, and conditions such as anxiety, autism, stress, and phobias are thought to be linked to its abnormal function". There is also growing evidence that the altered Amygdala acts and is "the mediator of the stress-dampening properties of alcohol". The Journal further stated, "alcohol-use disorders are also associated with negative reinforcing states", and in "individuals who drink alcohol to reduce anxiety or symptoms related to alcohol withdrawal." There is a causal relationship between anxiety and alcoholism.

The stress- dampening properties and effects of alcohol are easily recognized by anyone who pays keen attention to behavior and its derivative- spurt drinking. I have witnessed alcoholics drinking in spurts while adding recognition and celebratory qualities to their indulgence. It is customary to hear the exclamation, "I'll drink to that!" in response to a statement of accomplishment or during sports events. The alcoholic would always, in their own vernacular, say, "take a shot" or "fire one" or "one for the road" to answer the body's demand for alcohol without the thought process of voluntarily deciding to drink alcohol. Dr. Koob described this effect as "digging a hole every time you fix a hole".

Not to be forgotten is the effects of the BAL-blood alcohol level-which is a measurement of the percentage of alcohol in the blood that determines your individual cognitive response, as determined by accepted standards. To keep it simple, and to adhere to the National Institute of Alcohol Abuse & Alcoholism definition, in most states, a blood alcohol concentration of 0.08% defines an infraction of the law and an offense- intoxicated.

BAL increases when the volume of alcohol consumed increases, and that all behaviors, thoughts, and emotions are affected. Most people who consume excessively display behaviors that are very incongruous to their normal state of being. However, weight of the individual, and here we are talking about volume of water in the body, allows for the lowering of the BAL. A person whose weight is 200 pounds will show a lower BAL, after consuming eight beers, than a person who weighs 155 pounds.

Besides body weight, food plays an active role in determining BAL levels. Most knowledgeable drinkers intuitively know that an empty stomach cannot either dilute alcohol or slow down its absorption into the blood stream. As a result, such drinkers would eat high protein foods before drinking. Social drinkers, on the other hand, would mix alcohol with water or juices to slow down absorption into the blood stream.

Because the alcoholic integrates alcohol into his existence, the need for the presence of alcohol, not the volume, becomes important causing BAL readings to read higher. In the alcoholic, because of permanent changes, the need for rapid absorption takes center stage. The alcoholic's first drink is always a concentrated amount, measuring twice or more than would be consumed later. This required action contributes significantly to long term stomach problems.

To understand the insidious intrusion of concentrated alcohol into the stomach is to imagine sulfuric acid eroding a thin piece of cellophane paper. Similarly, alcohol erodes the stomach lining. The erosion produces a sticky mucous that the alcoholic must continuously expel. In addition to the erosion in the stomach, the pylorus valve, which connects the stomach and small intestine, goes into spasms when concentrated alcohol is present. This action-spasm- traps the alcohol in the stomach. The alcohol cannot move to the small intestine for absorption into the blood stream so it has no alternative but to be spread throughout the main body systems-brain, liver, heart, kidneys, lungs, and pancreas.

The heavy drinker finds himself, on an ongoing basis, having episodes of stomach discomfort and resorting to medications for relief. But, this continuous troubling stomach problems is not discomfort, it is simply stomach erosion brought about by excessive daily intake of alcohol. Yet, the alcoholic seeks only medical intervention for the stomach dysfunction and not for the permanency of metabolic adaptation in the liver and the permanency of molecular changes in the brain. He is fully aware that something is wrong, and continues seeking medical intervention from a clinician, who gives advice, but remains ambivalent in demanding action from the alcoholic. Such clinicians simply acquiesce to the alcoholic's requests for medications. The alcoholic is fully aware that the intervention he continues seeking only gives temporary relief. The alcoholic reflexively dismisses seeking help for dependency.

Excessive drinking which hospitalized many alcoholics every year convinced themselves that it was another condition that rendered them as candidates for hospitalization and observation. These alcoholics voluntarily accepted their dependency to themselves, while disassociating any relationship between the consumption of excessive alcohol and their ailments of the stomach.

A diminutive Asian male, who assumed a Latino heritage, comes to mind when thinking of those alcoholics, who continue to enter medical facilities to be treated for an assortment of stomach ailments, which have a direct relationship to alcohol abuse. I would call him Alberto, as in a bull I once knew, for his aggressive, confrontational, fearless, and daily belligerent behaviors. The years that follow, fit into every category of the compulsive dependent behaviors of the alcoholic that triggers physical altercations with everyone present. The alcohol propelled him to the status Zeus.

Alberto's physical confrontations were primarily targeted at his transient paramour. The latter reminded me of Janet, the tropical cyclone of 1955 that did damage to Aruba and Barbados. Alberto and Janet shared the commonality of addiction and dependency and damage to each other. They were aficionados of vodka. Occasionally, Alberto smoked crack cocaine while Janet popped pain killer medications, as if she were munching on pieces of fruit or candy. It was a remarkable sight!

I met Alberto, who at that time, was a pseudo superintendent of an apartment building with four floors and forty eight legal tenants- the actual number of residents was estimated by Alberto to be more than seventy-five. The building, throughout the years, had an influx of poor English and non-English emigrants and immigrants. Like everyone else, they jostled for housing, jobs, and a safer neighborhood for their families. Interestingly enough, they all shared the commonality of having one or two individuals from the numerous ethnic groups mingling with each other only during drinking sessions. It was only during drinking sessions, it seemed, that differences- language and culture- evaporated while the object of the gathering remained the same- alcohol.

It was known throughout the neighborhood that members of these impromptu groups would just appear one at a time, and coming from different directions. Most lived in adjacent communities away where congregating in front buildings was not tolerated. Meeting of the minds, as one member of the several groups termed their drinking sessions, took place on the sidewalk in front of any building where the air flow was tolerable. There was no set time for a drinking session to begin; it was nothing more than spontaneity dictated by dependency. Alcoholics, as the majority of congregants labeled themselves, just accepted the title to define their existence, after years of attempts at rehabilitation, and understood that their situation was functional.

Alberto had no official title indicating that he was the assigned superintendent of one of the many buildings, but all tenants assumed and gave acknowledgement to him as the caretaker. After all, Alberto dragged the twenty bins and pails filled with garbage and sorted the recyclables and placed them on the sidewalk for the sanitation twice weekly pick up. On occasion, he mopped the floors and applied hot wax to the delight of the residents. Yes, there was an official superintendent, but his whereabouts remained a mystery to all tenants. Nevertheless, he would appear whenever it was time for the annual building inspection or when there were electrical or plumbing problems in an apartment or somewhere in the building or subbasement where tenants were not allowed.

Janet owned a number of beauty parlors in the boroughs, where her primary customers were émigrés. As an ambitious immigrant woman, Janet saw the American dream through the eyes of her boyfriend, an immigrant from one of the Spanish speaking countries in the Caribbean. He was working long hours, which took him into the wee hours of the morning. He was tired from doing additional assignments. Nevertheless, he understood this was the path for upward mobility. He was determined to pass the certified public accounting examination. That piece of paper gave him professional legitimacy. He had the will and was on the fast track to fulfill his expectations. All he talked about was the advantage of youth and the opportunity that presented itself to him in America. He wanted to succeed, and that meant for him achieving- educationally and financially- like all those who came before him.

He had written a few, not so famous plays, which were funded by up- coming stars who were also on the fast track to stardom. He dabbled in the theatre district and kept his fulltime job in the financial district, as his security blanket and the conduit for financing future projects. He was ambitious and driven as opportunity presented itself.

Janet loved the theatre, and he, as a writer, who was well connected and known in a selected circle of actors complimented each other. Janet was supportive of him and accompanied him on tours when small groups of the not so famous were playing to the delight of the affluent crowds. She was known as a fixture that embraced all efforts he undertook. For her success or failure was not the issue. However, being an involved participant made the difference.

Janet's business was booming and prospects of expanding beyond her current locations were becoming a reality. She had made the right connections. After all, America is about hard work and good networking. Success became a reality when she opened three more beauty parlors and a designer clothing store. Janet described her climb up the ladder of success as, "flying high" when she purchased a Mercedes Benz 550S AMG. It was the ultimate display of material success. Things were going well for Janet.

A few months after Janet made her ultimate purchase, the love of her life was diagnosed with a progressively degenerating neuro-muscular disease. It was a sudden and devastating turn of events for him at that point in his life. According to Janet, he became depressed and began to drink vodka in large quantities after his diagnosis. Janet would also drink excessively a few days each week with him to provide the needed comfort that he deserved. He was going crazy after the diagnosis, and he became angry without provocation.

Alberto met Janet at the neighborhood spirits shop where he went to make another round of purchases- it was his third purchase for that evening. He was in a hurry to return to his drinking friends, but the long line with patrons was moving at the pace of a snail. Janet was in the line with spirits in one hand while rummaging with the other in her handbag for money to pay. Not only was she holding back customers who had double-parked their vehicles for a quick entry and exit, but also she was staggering from right to left causing patrons in front and behind her to feel uneasy. She was intoxicated and incoherent, yet in her hand were car keys with the escutcheon of the Mercedes Benz. This spelt danger!

For an unknown reason, Alberto came to her rescue by paying for the two bottles of spirits because he feared for her safety. He was also drinking, yet he saw danger in her actions and confident enough as he drove Janet to her destination. He parked the Mercedes and accompanied her to the entrance of the building where she lived. Janet opened the door and stumbled in without saying a word. This was the beginning of their relationship.

Weeks later she was making, as she termed it, pit stops at Alberto's place of residence to have a few drinks before going home to take care of her paramour. Janet enjoyed Alberto's carefree attitude and felt a compulsion to make a stop at his place. Despite Alberto's lack of cognitive skills or wealth or components to listen to music or anything else, there was an internal desire that propelled to be in his presence. Being there with him was all that mattered. These short intended stops became extended hours, and on occasion, became sleepovers because Janet was too drunk to find her way home.

Janet and Alberto became drinking partners, which progressed into sexual indulgences of another kind, as Alberto described their torrid and tumultuous relationship over the years. I never found out what he meant by another kind to describe his prowess sexual proclivities. But it was more than that because their relationship was engulfed with physical violence against each other. Alberto always rationalized his physical assaults as, keeping her in check. Alberto believed, and for good reason, that she was jeopardizing his sojourn and unlawful residence within the space he occupied and claimed as home. He was nervous whenever she drank too much. Tenants complained that Janet was always boisterous and sometimes physical and confrontational during drinking sessions with Alberto. Everyone, over time, became aware of her histrionics and avoided her like a plague.

Alberto was reprimanded for her behaviors by tenants and by the official superintendent. The latter requested that Janet not be on the premises or in the confines of the location, which Alberto used as his place of abode. For him, at that time, she was a liability. Alberto knew and understood that his position as a pseudo superintendent was not acknowledged, by the owners of the buildings, yet he had place of abode.

Alberto occupied a room in the subbasement that was hidden away and accessible to maintenance personnel. A large bed, a few old chairs, a dining table, and his belongings stacked in boxes. Both of his overcoats were hung behind on nails affixed to the door. There was no bathroom or kitchen or adequate ventilation. A large industrial fan kept the air circulating and forcing its way into the ventilating system. Nevertheless, the refrigerator had frozen foods. Because of the paucity of sanitation, Janet's presence in this confined location caused concern for the absent building superintendent.

Despite warnings from the building superintendent and reprimands by Alberto, Janet continued visiting Alberto on a regular basis. Janet confessed that she was drinking more frequently and passing out after each marathon session and not returning to her residence. Alberto enjoyed her frequent visits. She had the finances while he struggled and needed his daily indulgences. He was caught in a difficult situation, and had to be disingenuous when he reprimanded Janet for being verbally obnoxious on the premises. She had the keys to what he needed, and believed that if he kept her silent during her visits things would be tolerable for everyone. He described that arrangement as "pissing in the wind"; Janet defied all ultimatums to keep way from the residence.

Janet was now becoming intoxicated everyday beginning in the morning, just minutes after the neighborhood liquor store opened. She started paying less attention to her business; denying him of the support, she once gave him; robbed by drinking associates who frequented Alberto's residence; paying limited attention to her appearance and general decorum. Janet was transformed into a female whose thought process was hidden in a bottle.

He was on his own to take care of his physical needs. He was also drinking beyond his tolerance. His medical condition limited him from doing those things he normally would do. He lacked the ability to make the trip to the liquor store. Nevertheless, he got what he wanted and became profusely generous with tips given to persons who purchased his daily fill of spirits. He lost interest in Janet and sought comfort in the bottle. Janet continued providing intermittent assistance to him while spending the greater part of her day with Alberto drinking to the point of stupor.

A few years later, after drinking all day she was struck by a car while trying to cross a major street. She suffered three fractured ribs, a broken left leg, and lacerations about the body, a broken jaw, and injuries to her lower back. She spent four weeks in the hospital with excruciating pains that could only be treated with

Hydrocodone 7.5-200mg. Janet's journey into legal addiction started.

She was discharged and stockpiled with an assortment of pain alleviating pharmaceuticals. Janet remained in pain as she adhered to the regiment of painkiller pills. Within a short period, Janet was medicating herself with incremental amounts of her prescribed Hydrocodone pills to be relieved of the pains she experienced throughout the day. But, Janet was not only medicating herself with Hydrocodone, she continued drinking at the same pace she did before her accident. Within a month Janet returned to her physician for continued therapy of Hydrocodone-, she received 120 pills. Janet was now ADDICTED TO PILLS.

She became fully aware of her newly acquired addiction and dependency, and sought interventions. Thus begun Janet's involvement and attempts at rehabilitation at a few hospitals, where she completed detoxification numerous times, but failed to follow through with the other phases needed to maintain sobriety. She felt in charge.

Within weeks of her discharge, Janet was having a drink. She admitted to having a drink or two because she felt like having a drink, and that she understood the implications. Janet viewed detoxification as the method to free the system of impurities, while relegating after care as less important for her continued sobriety. She accepted her new status as being changed from the inside permanently.

Janet was killed in an automobile accident while crossing the street. She was drunk. Alberto succumbed to complications from COPD and excessive consumption of alcohol.

Most alcoholics, like those mentioned, are very resistant to the counseling approach, yet indulged in perfunctory sessions. All abusers were very receptive to therapeutic approaches that balances the freedom to indulge and without imposing demands. They wanted to have it both ways, until their indulgence gets to the point where they cannot abstain, because of the permanent and irreversible changes that have taken place. Pharmacology fits the requests of many who do not attribute their dependency to psychological problems.

THE CORTICORTROPIN RELEASE FACTOR (CRF)

The brain does experience stress.

One chemical that is found to play a significant, if not the significant role, in how the brain's stress response system works is called the CRF (corticotrophin releasing factor). This chemical is naturally produced by the brain. Simply put, CRF springs into action when there is immediate stress present, such as deadlines, academic finals, a physical examination, or when illness is perceived or presents itself. The CRF, in a basic way, is very similar to the gag reflex that is triggered when you are being chocked or the scratch response to an itch. It is the body's way of saying calm down and you need something to bring you back in balance. The brain, therefore, creates the natural chemical- CRF- as a response to handle whatever stressful situation is present, by returning the brain to its normal activities. It is the body's natural chemical mechanism for the alleviation of stress.

It is interesting to note that CRF, which is designed and naturally produced by the body, for its calming effect, is unnaturally triggered by alcohol and drug use. Alcohol and pharmaceutically manufactured drugs, on the other hand, are unnatural and, as such, cannot be produced by the body while CRF is a natural chemical made by the body. When the externally unnatural chemicals are in the body, the unnatural act of firing CRF begins. Alcohol like external drugs ingested into the system propels the involuntary chemical release of CRF by the brain. It is this unnatural and unregulated release of CRF fueling dependence. Take notice that there are two forces at work- one voluntarily and one involuntarily- which are influenced when alcohol or drugs are present in the body. It is important to understand that alcohol, which has already done irreparable damage, remains the agent in control of the response of CRF in the Amygdala.

As was stated, CRF helps the brain to return to its normal activity after a heightened sensation of pleasure. However, years of heavy drinking or drug taking make the brains become more sensitive to CRF and causes CRF to be spontaneously released continuously whenever alcohol is present in the system. The continuous firing of CRF has nothing to do with the volume of alcohol. Rather, it is the presence of alcohol in the system that creates the reaction. Remember, the irreversible and permanent structural changes that have already taken place in the brains of the alcoholic and drug abuser have alcohol to maintain functionality. Psychological issues are not dominant although they play a role in the lives of abusers. Rather, it is the molecular changes and metabolic adaptation combined, which neither the alcoholic nor the drug abuser has any control over anytime. Those permanent molecular changes cause demands that feed the CRF with alcohol or drugs. These demands dictate behavior. Psychotherapy cannot change behavior that is now dictated by permanent chemical changes, but can only provide tools to assist the abuser to remain stable.

[24]Paul Kenny, who studied the molecular underpinnings of addiction, at the Icahn School of Medicine at Mount Sinai, stated that the brain remembers that CRF relieves stress and its response to stress becomes "stuck in high gear". The CRF just keeps firing and demanding alcohol as its source fuel. CRF, stuck in high gear, as we can refer to the process, caused by alcohol and drug abuse, is now referred to as the "misery neurotransmitter". The latter is thought to be the ingredient that causes anxiousness felt by addicts and alcoholics, until they receive temporary relief by drinking again or taking drugs. CRF is considered as "the driver behind the

difficulties that alcoholics or addicts have trying to quit". The CRF is the proverbial two-edged sword.

[24] The Misery Neurotransmitter, CRF, which causes the anxiety of addicts, and which keeps them locked into their habits, needs serious investigation. According to Markus Heilig, clinical director at the NIAAA, a part of the National Institutes of Health, early-stage testing in alcoholics with experimental drugs, such as gabapentin, that aims to stop CRF from revving up the brain's stress centers, are being conducted. The results are striking and remarkable!

Gabapentin has been used by researchers on several controlled groups for years. One group of 150 alcoholics was monitored for a number of years by Dr. Mason. The results from this and other controlled groups of 150 alcoholics were surprising. Dr. Mason's JAMA published studies of this group of alcoholics, 98% of those who took the highest dose of gabapentin either stopped drinking altogether or did so occasionally. This success led researchers and the NIAAA to continue testing gabapentin on heroin addicts.

Gabapentin, known by the brand name Neurontin, is a mood stabilizer in those with bipolar disorder. It has the same minimal side effects. However, gabapentin, when used to treat alcoholics specifically, the results were stunning. The Journal of Clinical Psychology stated that "gabapentin reduces alcohol consumption and cravings, which help patients to maintain sobriety", and concurred with other studies in JAMA that other approaches to treating addiction must be considered and used for clinical intervention. Interestingly enough, JAMA in January 2014, indicated that only 9% of U.S alcoholics use drugs such as gabapentin. The Scripps Research Institute, Pearson Center for Alcoholism & Addiction Research, La Jolla, California, supports the findings on gabapentin.

The discussion and research on alcoholism and drug addiction continue to move in another direction and beyond the psychological. It is showing promising results in pharmaceutical approaches. This is in no way an endorsement of Gabapentin, but it clearly demonstrates that another approach, by pharmaceuticals for the interdiction of alcohol dependency and drug addiction.

HEROIN & PRESCRIBED NARCOTICS PILLS

Recently, the resurgence of heroin, after a decline in the 1990's, has resurfaced in a new generation; created indirectly by physicians and pain management experts. When examined carefully, we see that the widespread prescription drug abuse of the 1990's triggered a surge in prices for abusers, leading those with minimal finances to the much cheaper heroin.

Heroin is now the choice for those who became addicted to pain medications. Addiction crept in legally, while the satisfaction for pain medications was dictated by an increasing need for a dosage higher than was prescribed, but could not be afforded by the addict because of the prohibitive prices in the illegal market. The truth simple-heroin is now used by persons who are addicted to legal prescription narcotics. Most users attribute their addicted behaviors to medical malpractice that paved the path for their dependency, and pointed the finger directly at clinicians who simply wrote a prescription mechanically.

Three facts, as follows:

1. Prescribed pains killer narcotics have led to addiction for patients under the medical care and supervision of clinicians. And, for those whom addiction is the by-product of a legal drug, dependency goes beyond what dosage was prescribed.

2. Patients are now doubling their intake of prescribed drugs by purchasing additional pills on the black market where prices have escalated.
3. Current pain killer narcotic medications, which are legal for those it was prescribed, have become too expensive for those addicted to, but were not prescribed the drugs.

I pointed out earlier that many abusers felt that medical providers, and in particular, the general practitioner, responds to treating pain in a proactive and crisis management style by writing a prescription; without doing a thorough analysis of the patient. Like the general practitioner, medical pain specialists are also guilty by responding to the verbally disingenuous pleas from patients for relief from ostensibly excruciating pain. For the physician, relief from pain is of paramount importance. It is the acquiescing by clinicians that has laid the groundwork for continued indulgences. By extension, it facilitates involuntary addiction, and dependency.

All abusers, despite laying some of the blame on clinicians, stated that there was an internal propensity to increase their dosage despite knowing and understanding the long term ramifications. Only a few attributed their propensity to consume illicit substances as an addiction. A great numbers attributed their propensity to use or abuse drugs or alcohol as dependency. All complained about the financial and the personal costs from their abuse of substances.

Many prescription drug addicts verified that their daily use and habit required 20 to 30 pills, depending on the potency. Most stated that the escalating cost factor was becoming unsustainable, as prices per pill escalated to a high of $30. Addicts were stuck with a daily bill averaging $500. Because of the escalating costs, addicts admitted that economics kicked in immediately and price and availability became the only considerations. The substitution rule became the alternative. The alternative became heroin.

In the City of Newark, New Jersey, heroin is rampantly sold at half the price and discounts are available compared to the prices paid within the five boroughs of New York City. Newark is now considered the trading center where buyers and sellers congregate to transact retail and wholesale purchases. Some people even refer to Newark as "The Exchange" similar to The Stock Exchange, for financial transactions.

Baddas, whom I spoke about in an earlier chapter, described the frenzy for heroin in Newark as simply stunning. I learned that people were taking commuter planes and going there only to purchase heroin. Newark, considered by many as the epicenter of illicit activities, also attracts persons in wheel chairs, walkers, and canes to satisfy their thirst for heroin. Newark was bustling and thriving with heroin activities and with boldness that outstripped all prior activities in illicit substances. He believed that the carefree trade in illicit substances resulted from the demands of the new pool of addicts.

In New York City, the borough of Staten Island, away from its bucolic past, and punctuated by a history of political decisions on ending landfills, tells another story. Staten Island, once a sleepy enclave of the five boroughs, made up of a collection of small communities totaling some 470,000, has awakened to demographic, political, racial, and social changes.

Staten Islanders are awakening to the reality that their communities are no longer insulated from the ravages that affected the adjacent communities of New York City throughout the past two decades. Residents are now awakening to a new assault that has taken place with the speed of lightening. The assault has infested all neighborhoods in the borough. It is no longer considered, as many say "not in my back yard". The reality- the world is changing and heroin has arrived.

Staten Island's location, and by extension, proximity and accessibility to Newark, New Jersey, became ideal for all kinds of illegal activities. Location is everything. Staten Island is the conduit that gives quick accessibility to other states in the south and eastern seaboard of the United States.

The New York Times makes the point when it stated, "For decades, heroin was mostly found in the northern section of the island where the ferry docks from Manhattan and the Verrazano-Narrows Bridge touches down from Brooklyn" where it was contained and isolated. This northern section of Staten Island, the boroughs poorest and densely populated by minorities, became the established open-air supermarket for illicit drugs of all kinds within the housing developments of Stapleton, Park Hill, and Tottenville. Illicit activities in the aforementioned developments were concentrated and known to the local constabulary whose efforts at disrupting drug sales and supplies were meaningless, while residents became marginalized and associated with lesser than human ethics, morals, or values.

Illicit drugs were seen ages ago as a Black and Latino problem that could be contained, managed, and even overlooked. It was then concentrated in those areas, as they are today, and bringing indelible grief and ravages to the working class communities. The more affluent white communities remained insulated and protected. Politicians and elected officials reinforced the isolation of the African American and Latino communities by appealing to racial feelings, but could not keep at bay the indulgences of a new generation of whites who explored the bowels of the bygone forbidden sections of the borough in search of their fix. The addiction and dependency on pain killer narcotics are now endemic in the Caucasian communities of Staten Island.

Today's illicit drug activities are, and must be, the concern of every community or it will become like a roach infestation that can only be contained and not eradicated. We must not revert to an era where eminent scholars like Timothy Leary, American psychologist, who was part of Harvard Psilocybin Project, advocated psychedelic drugs to assist in psychotherapy. Dr. Leary was famous for this proposal and became associated with terms like Turn on; Tune in; Drop out.

Staten Island is 64 % white, according to the 2010 census. This population is concentrated in the sleepy bedroom communities of Oakwood, Great Kills, and Eltingville, to name a few. In these communities pain killing drugs like Roxicodone, Vicodin, and Percocet have proliferated in the adult population and is beginning to gain root in the adolescent population. Because of increased demands for pain killers and a paucity of finances to satisfy the demands, bartering is now in vogue within these communities.

A few people are now trading haircuts in exchange for pain medications, while others are doing whatever it takes to satisfy their insatiable appetite for these drugs. It symbolizes and gives life to the 2012 rap song titled Pain killer paradise, Staten Island by a group called White Trash Clan. The referencing by the latter group was to show the dangers of these PILLS, and its effects when the lyrics stated emphatically that using Pills, would cause you, "to literally end up in jail, or the fucking gutters, or worst," according to the producer of the group. One girl from the group of video stars was recently arrested in a drug bust in 2013 for selling drugs to an undercover agent. There you go with Pills!

Remember, the world is changing as is the image of the heroin user changing, yet many are stuck in time and have their heads buried and insular and indifferent to change. The great majority of heroin users are now white men and women who mostly live outside the cities. Recent research published in JAMA of Psychiatry tracked 2,800 heroin users and found that first-time users are now generally older than those who began taking the drug in the 1960's. About 90 percent are white and 75% are now living in non-urban areas according to the published 2014 study. The research further confirmed a link between the rise of opioid abuse and the growing use of heroin. The National Survey on Drug Use and Health stated that heroin use jumped 80% from 2007 to 2012 to a mind boggling 669,000 known users. Let us take a brief economics and history lesson.

During the 1990's, heroin use declined significantly in the United States,while there was a geometric increase in the demand- legally and illegally- for pain killers. As demand outstripped the accessibility and supply of pain killers beyond what was prescribed by a physician, all prices rose quickly. For those who were not prescribed pain killers but were addicted to them, accessibility became prohibitively expensive because there was a two tier process in obtaining a continuous supply.

Heroin arrived because of the laws of economics; demand and supply and substitution effects influence pricing. Economics will dictate decisions once demand is established and propelled by needs and wants. The commodity, pain medication, coupled with addiction creates a need that must be satisfied. As we talked about earlier, the purveyors and creators of this need- clinicians and pharmaceutical companies- must be assigned the blame for their compliance with satisfying the need/s of abusers.

Demand and Economic Substitution effects are at work. The substitution effect causes addicts to substitute relatively lower-priced goods, heroin, for the relatively higher-priced pain killer medication when prices go up. It is that simple. Gil Kerlikowske, the White House drug czar, makes the connection by stating, "pain-killer addicts have switched to heroin as pills became too expensive or less accessible." The addict is now faced with the dilemma of his demands for the narcotic pain killers beyond his disposable income. His demands are driven by addiction and controlled by limited finances. Both controlling forces will always dictate submission to purchase the less expensive.

The heroin dealer, on the other hand, faced with increases in production and supply of high potency of heroin from Mexico, which needs to be in the veins and arteries of the addicted as quickly as possible. He has quality and quantity, but needs to build a consumer base and brand loyalty, as heroin is sold under different names and associated with the retailer. The dealer must also be seen as the marketer, and as one who sees an opportunity to saturate and gain market share, by using the increases in production, which created an increase in supply in the short run and with no change in potency. Thus, the lower price of heroin gives the addict only one option, make the purchase of the less expensive yet addictive drug to satisfy addiction. The producers of poppy have increased production and supply without altering potency, while implicitly creating, for the addict, a better allocation of disposable income for their purchases. It is the genius of marketing at work.

The increases in supply, which saturate the market in the short run with fixed demand of heroin, causes a decrease in the price and at the same time, open the gates of addiction for new consumers, who were previously using narcotic painkillers that have now become prohibitively expensive. A new consumer pool is thus created.

This new consumer pool compromises both the legally prescribed recipient, who now needs additional dosage, and the consumer who is addicted to pain killers. As demand increases, while supply is constant, price rises. Because prices for pain medication have adhered to the economic laws of supply and demand coupled with income and substitution effects, in the classical style, where demand outstrips supply, prices would rise geometrically. In the long run, this new consumer pool pays more, not only financially, but emotionally, and by extension the financial costs inflicted upon society as a whole becomes burdensome. Once again, the laws of economics are at work.

According to the DEA (Drug Enforcement Agency), the rising level of heroin in use in recent years stems from "a corresponding epidemic in the abuse of prescription opiate-based painkillers, such as oxycodone". And, since a direct correlation has been made between a legally prescribed narcotic and a resurgent in the use of an illegally obtained substance- heroin-it seems that the medical community needs to share in the blame of addiction and dependency.

Yes, the medical community must share in the blame for addiction. Go into Duane Reade, Rite Aid, CVS, or any of the national chain of pharmacies, and it boggles the mind to find a chemical portion for everything from the common cold, containing addictive substances, to hemorrhoids. It's the over-the- counter drugs mentality of promises to "change the way you feel", as some posted advertisement states, coupled with the familiar "Say No to Drugs" campaign, during a prior administration, seems in contradiction, as we appeal for a drug at the local pharmacy to take us through the day or to sleep at night. These drugs, as innocuous as they seem and appealing through social media formats, can be used to get high, and are used to get high, because they are easily available throughout the nation and approved by the FDA.

What makes it more interesting is that even prescription drugs are advertised on television, magazines, billboards, subways cars throughout the nation, and most recently, the buyers of over-the-counter medications are encouraged to do their own diagnosis and prescribing while in the drug stores. One can now enter any chain pharmacy, observe several charts with questions, and answers like Do you have a headache. Take 500 milligrams of---- and the drug is named. Do you have severe cramps? Take 200 milligrams of----and again, the drug is named. There are questions and answers for almost every ailment.

Recently, to add further insult to injury, the medical community has embraced a new formulation of Oxycodone which has a 12-hour time release. In nonprofessional terms, "it's a long high". Yet, the pharmaceutical companies were not satisfied with profits, and they were substantial, from Oxycontin. In the name of greed, they went further to produce Hydrocodone, which is sold under the name Vicodin, and once again, supported by the medical community. Both are in cahoots to maximize profits at the expense of addiction.

The medical practitioners in conjunction with pharmaceutical companies and sales representatives have become supportive of pain medications, such as Subsys, despite having knowledge of their negative and addictive effects. [27]According to the New York Times article by Katie Thomas, former sales representative from Insys that manufactures Subsys, the company is now "aggressively marketing" the painkiller to oncologists. Katie Thomas further stated that the aggressive marketing of Subsys also included physicians who did not treat any cancer patient or many cancer patients. According to her, it was simply marketing of a product that pays "higher commissions for selling higher doses of the drug". It became profits before people.

In a follow up article she pointed out that a Connecticut "advanced practice registered nurse", who was authorized to prescribe medication to patients, allegedly received kickbacks – $83,000- from Insys Therapeutics. Shocking as it seemed, this nurse was responsible for more than $1,000,000 in Medicare claims.

Most of the patients who received the medication did not have a diagnosis for cancer.

The FDA continues to do the waltz with Subsys by applying disingenuous methods called directives to guide certified practitioners- oncologists and pain specialist- authorized to prescribe this specific medication. Despite granting the license specifically to oncologists, who treat persons with cancer, and to pain specialist who do not treat cancer patients, the power to issue a prescription to the sufferer of pain and not cancer, rests in the hands of all pain specialist and not in the hands of the oncologist. Once again, it is marketing and profits, and a product for all to exploit.

This regulation places Subsys, a pain killer, directly into the hands of those persons addicted to narcotic-painkillers. It is simply done through the prescription pads of the pain specialists who do not treat cancer patients. Subsys, which is a form of Fentanyl, has been described as, "a narcotic that is used when painkillers like morphine fail to provide relief". Subsys fits that description. Subsys, manufactured by Insys Therapeutics, was approved in 2012, but it was only approved specifically for cancer patients who were already using "round-the-clock painkillers".

So, in order for the patient to be prescribed Subsys, according to the FDA, he or she needs to meet the following : already be on prescribed pain medication/s that is being used round-the clock ; treated specifically by an oncologist(not a pain specialist or any licensed practitioner/ medical doctor) before Subsys can be prescribed. Yet in 2013, according to Symphony Heath, which analyses drug trends, only 1% of the prescriptions written for Subsys were written by oncologists. It seems that anyone who has the title MD is now writing a prescription for Subsys. Medical doctors are not all the same.

Because of this new phenomenon of addiction, created by pain specialists, there were significant increases in demand, legally and illegally for Subsys, causing prices to increase for other prescription drugs. While the demands for pain killer medications were increasing, countries like, Afghanistan, Mexico, Latin American countries, and Columbia were having bumper crops of opium poppy because of better production methods, and this was becoming the norm causing prices to drop for illegal heroin.

According to the Substance Abuse and Mental Health Services Administration, 80% of people trying heroin for the first time previously used prescription pain drugs. It has been estimated that heroin users in the United States have jumped almost 80% to 669,000 in 2012, up from 373,000 in 2007. At the same time, the annual overdose death attributed to heroin hit 3,094 in 2010, an increase of 55% since 2000, as per the Centers for Disease Control and Prevention.

Because of increased demands for heroin coupled with a 45% increase of heroin deaths- 3,038 in 2010- the Attorney General, Eric Holder, in 2014, called this occurrence an "urgent public health crisis". He stated that his agency was stepping up efforts to "stem sharp increases in deadly heroin overdoses and to interrupt trafficking in the drug and abuse of prescription narcotics". The Federal Government has taken action, not to interdict the distribution of illegal and addictive drugs, but to save the lives of those who overdose.

Because saving lives has now become a mantra, political forces, such as the Federal Government has called for all enforcement agencies to train and equip personnel with a medication called naloxone, which reverses the effects of an overdose. Many municipalities, including New York City, have given out naloxone kits to all emergency personnel to decrease ongoing incidents of death from overdoses.

Alcohol and cocaine abuse and overdoses are nothing new. Such incidents are happening every day in communities throughout the nation without public fanfare or outcries. However, when famous actors /musicians and personalities succumb to alcohol and drug abuses the nation takes note. Whitney Huston, Heath Ledger, Marilyn Monroe, Elvis Presley, Michael Jackson, John Montief, Anna Nicole Smith, and Philip Seymour Hoffman deaths were indelible in the minds of the nation, and are testimony to substance abuses that transcends geographic boundaries, and every lifestyle.

We should not forget Jimmy Hendrix and Janis Joplin who also succumbed to heroin deaths. But the most shocking death from heroin that paints a hedonistic and devastating picture is a son succumbing to death by heroin that was provided by his biological mother. John Simon Richie aka Sid Vicious of the group called the Sex Pistols was such a person. Vicious was supplied his daily doses of heroin and paraphernalia by his mother since he was young. Vicious died at age 21 in the West Village of New York City.

The deaths of Jimmy Hendrix and Janis Joplin and Sid Vicious were the by-product of the 60's and 70's era of indulgences. Artists, musicians, and people in the arts manifested the sordid effects of addiction, yet the urban poor took the blame. The five boroughs of New York City have once again, become infested with heroin.

Heroin has always been viewed as an urban scourge throughout the 1960's and up to the 1980's, and an affliction of the poor whose finances were meager. Yet, the indulgence of the poor seeped into the counter- culture existence of the radicals and artists during the Vietnam era. Theodore Cicero, vice chairperson for research at Washington University School of Medicine in St. Louis, stated, "Heroin is not confined to inner-city areas" and has become the choice in suburban and rural communities and brought with it the ravages of addiction of a prior period.

According to the FDA, a dose of heroin in 1980 was about 5% pure, but today it is not uncommon for purity to be 50%, and as such, making it potentially more lethal. More troubling, is the combination of heroin with the deadly synthetic drug called Fentanyl that has resulted in 37 deaths in Maryland and 22 in Pennsylvania. In 2013, 464 deaths, while there was 428 in the first 9 months of 2014 in Maryland.

With such alarming statistics attributed to heroin use and abuse, there is a need for an international approach whereby heroin remains a product that is controlled by government for its intended use as a pain killer, as is morphine, which is a derivative from opium. Economically punitive actions should become the bargaining chip in the war on heroin, and for nations violating any international treaty and agreement for the production, distribution, and control of the product.

The USA must take the leadership role, in conjunction with efforts by the International Monetary Fund and the World Bank, in making their lending and assistance contingent on countries adhering to poppy crops production, with enforcement, to stymie the flow of heroin into all nations.

It is time that we act as a unified force in the battle of drug addiction and alcohol dependency.

SUBSTANCE ABUSE BY OLDER ADULTS

One sector of the population that is overlooked when we speak of drug addiction is the aging population, and particularly the aged. The latter continues to be seen, not as substance abusers, despite clinicians and the public recognizing that this population is susceptible to self-medication. We continue to see the aged population as individuals who are dependent on medications to alleviate pain, which comes with the aging process. It becomes the process of keeping this sector of the population alive with pills and other forms of medication.

In 2008, it was reported that 231,200 people over 50 sought treatment for substance abuse. It was further estimated in 2012 that one in 1,000 seniors, abuse or are addicted to illicit drugs, according to the Substance Abuse and Mental Health Services Administration, a federal agency. Not to anyone's surprise, with the frequency and quick fix medical approaches to providing instant relief, seniors are progressing and becoming the new pool of addicts. According to the Addiction Journal, it was estimated that 2.8 million older adults, comprising of senior citizens and those over 50 years old, in the United States of America, meet the criteria for alcohol abuse, as of 2013, and this represents 6% of adults between the ages of 50 to 64 who are indulging in illicit drug use.

Troublesome is the projection for those over 50 years old in 2020. An alarming estimate of 5.7 million older adults will meet the criteria for alcohol abuse by that time. As we get older, and it is no secret, and spoken by those who are alcoholics and drug addicts, it takes longer for our bodies to metabolize alcohol and drugs. Bluntly put, the body can no longer handle and process the continuous intrusion of alcohol, licit and illicit drugs.

The driving force behind alcoholism and drug abuse in older adults is rooted in the following: boredom, loneliness, depression, lack of passion for anything, lack of engagement, and an apprehension to engage in volunteer activities. All the aforementioned factors, not excluding psychological and psychiatric issues, fuel the urge to medicate with alcohol or drugs. The taking of numerous medications has now become an exercise without any consideration for the future effects because it was prescribed by the physician. Because of this approach, many older adults are addicted to drugs like Klonopin, an anti-anxiety medication, Ambien, for sleeping issues, and a host of pain killer medications like, Hydrocodone, OxyContin, and Percocet.

The very physicians who prescribed these addictive drugs, are being asked, through medical guidelines, to tests their patients to make sure that patients are neither abusing pills nor failing to take them. This edict came about because of abusive billings submitted to Medicaid and Medicare. These new guidelines to medical providers were intended to make them impotent and to surrender to the dictates of those who held the financial purses. It became comply or die. The alternative for the medical practitioner was to offset costs involved in satisfying guidelines established by the federal government. The simple urine test became the conduit to meet guidelines, which became the lifeline for the practitioner.

A new and a very profitable industry developed to satisfy another mandate, under governmental control, because of these new directives. It was back to square one with additional regulations, but with ammunition for the benefit of the practitioner. Pain specialists are now given the tools to, once more, extract additional funds from Medicaid, and on occasion, directly from patients.

Because of this new development- high-tech, profitable testing methods with fewer billing restrictions- seniors must be attuned and vigilant. Seniors must know why; what they were tested and the compensation by Medicare for physicians.

MARIJUANA IN TODAY'S CHANGING WORLD

From the Marijuana Tax Act of 1937, followed by the Narcotics Control Act of 1956, when severe penalties were mandatory for the possession of marijuana, the mood of the nation has now changed favoring legalization. Colorado, Washington State, Oregon, Alaska, and the District of Columbia led the nation in 2014, with legal sales of marijuana for recreational purposes.

Since Colorado and three other states started this approach, and succeeded in making marijuana legal for recreational use for those 21 and over, 23 other, states and the District of Columbia have decriminalized marijuana for medical reasons. Alaska and Oregon, like California, are now moving forward, by using ballot initiatives to promote and build momentum to legalize marijuana use, but not in public places or accommodations.

As the universal momentum is building for the decriminalization of marijuana, 58% of the public in the United States of America are supportive of legalization. At the same time, state representatives are plotting and are being wooed by industry power brokers to truncate decriminalization, which is supported in some states, to reflect the majority choice for Federal legalization and uniformity throughout the country, despite the sovereignty of each state. Such an approach does not negate state rights, but gives rights, and does not create an imbalance with laws or contradicting each other state by state. It gives freedom of choice.

The mood of the nation now views decriminalization as wrapped up illegality, for future prosecution; because of federal laws making marijuana possession, a felony is still enforced. The nation, according to Gallop polls, is favoring legalization, as was done after prohibition of alcohol ended with the ratification of the 21st amendment, which repealed the 18th amendment in 1933.

Canada, our northern neighbor, on the other hand, has not only decriminalized marijuana, but moved swiftly to national legalization that gives approval of its use to everyone in need. Canada is now seeking overseas purchases of marijuana for consumers and patients, and has become progressively more adventurous and daring in their appealing and creative marketing approaches to gain allegiance. The Indie film company, known as A24, has struck a deal with a Los Angeles medical-marijuana dispensary called Buds & Roses to sell two new cannabis strains- Mr. Tusk and White Walrus. The former strain is more intense while the latter is milder.

As the northern hemisphere continues to support legalization, Cambodia and North Korea have already legalized marijuana. On December 10, 2013, marijuana was legalized in Uruguay. It is interesting to note the reason given and stated by officials in Uruguay, for the legalization of marijuana for export, was that "economics dictated decisions" for foreign exchange earnings. Many other foreign countries such as Mexico, Paraguay, St. Vincent and the Grenadines, and Jamaica are having bountiful crop production. While their economies are struggling, Thier thinking has evolved, marijuana is no longer an illegal drug but an earning commodity which has international demands. Here we see countries looking for viable alternatives, and in this case marijuana as part of their economic structure. Legalizing of marijuana as an export commodity will yield foreign exchange returns.

Israel, on the other hand, sees marijuana through another set of lenses. The Holy Land has made a spiritual connection and a responsibility to a higher power to be benevolent, and marijuana, despite its illegality as a (dangerous?) drug, is endorsed for its good. The government has approved medical marijuana farms to be grown in specific locations, with state of the art equipment for controlling light and humidity, as is done in the Safed area, a center of Jewish mysticism. To add the religious component, there is an on-site synagogue at these locations, as symbols of Tikkun Olam, which reinforces the Jewish concept of healing and repairing the world.

Because of Israel's lack of legislation regulating marijuana for medicinal purposes, the innovative spirit of its people, once more, came alive. Prof. Raphael Mechoulam and Yechiel Gaoni at Weizmann Institute of Science, in the 1990's, isolated, analyzed, and synthesized the main psychoactive ingredient in marijuana, THC. The result of their work, synthesizing, produced a strain called Eran Almog, which has the highest concentration of THC, and is recommended for severe pain.

While numerous countries have decriminalized and legalized marijuana, pronouncements persist that marijuana is addictive, causes cognitive deficiencies, and that dependency develops over time. Such claims, painted with a broad brush, and juxtaposed with contradictory information only add more confusion to the issue of marijuana in contemporary society.

It should be made crystal clear that that the effects of marijuana on the adolescent brains, which are not fully developed, differ from the adult brains, and are susceptible to cognitive deficiencies when marijuana is used. A 2012 study published in the Proceedings of the National Academy of Science, showed teenagers in New Zealand who smoked marijuana heavily experienced an IQ drop of up to 8 points. It must also be emphasized that marijuana has contributing effects on the lungs and heart, as alcohol and tobacco- legal products- with highly addictive and dependency propensities.

In places like New York City, we can easily observe persons addicted to nicotine, the main ingredient in cigarettes, smoking as they walk down the streets or exit their places of employment to take a cigarette break, and legally permitted every few hours. Their addictions are on public display and without any negative ramifications for such actions. It is allowed and implicitly encouraged by employers to avoid the label of discrimination by those who abhor smoking.

When Michael Bloomberg became mayor of New York City in 2002, the city's adult smoking population stood at 21.5%, and under his stewardship declined to a low 14% in 2010. After Bloomberg left office, city officials reported that the adult smoking population rate rose to 16.1% in 2013, and this growth rate took place across all ages, ethnic and racial groups despite numerous efforts in print and visual media personalizing the negative effects of smoking. However, on the national level, cigarette smoking decreased. During Mayor Bloomberg's tenure, he successfully pushed for banning smoking in parks, beaches, and other public places including in front of any city buildings. The Mayor fought for, and raised the minimum age for purchasing cigarettes from 18 to 21, but forgot that adults can make purchases for teenagers and that there is easy access to cigarettes in the illicit market throughout the boroughs. All efforts, including television campaigns like, Imagine for Life, that depicts the devastating effects of smoking, have failed to make any significant impact on the 64.9% of city smokers who tried to quit at least once. Public awareness of the dangers of cigarette smoking has had little impact on adolescent behavior.

In Denver, Colorado, public health officials have taken unorthodox methods to warn teenagers of the dangers of smoking either tobacco cigarettes or marijuana, but not the combination of both. Warning signs with bold headings such as; 'Does Marijuana really cause schizophrenia in teenagers? Smoke and Find Out.', 'Subjects Needed, Must be a teenager! Must smoke weed! Must have 8 IQ Points to Spare.', are nothing more than bandaids, carrying little cognitive or visual effect beyond an initial attention grabber. Such approaches, although seemingly directed to trigger some thought on the negative aspects of smoking, have had little effect on adolescent behavior which is greatly influenced by peer pressure.

It is an established fact that in the adolescent, pleasure-seeking is sought while risk- taking behaviors becomes the challenges that are wrapped up in a sense of invincibility and exploration. The years of adolescence present the challenges that make vulnerability, leading to addiction, a quick transition. It is not marijuana in its pure and unadulterated form that is demonstrably addictive, but the known addictive properties of nicotine that brings about the addiction and propels the dependency.

Dr. Mitchell S. Rosenthal, child psychiatrist, and founder of Phoenix House, makes the point of seemingly invincibility by the youth by stating that when you, "link adolescent pleasure –seeking and risk-taking to marijuana's impairment of perception and judgment, it isn't surprising that a 2004 study of seriously injured drivers in Maryland found that half the teens tested positive for marijuana". His focus was on cognition and impairment, and how the latter translates into negative behaviors, and not addiction.

Dr. Nora Volker, director of the National Institute on Drug Abuse, when talking about adolescent behavior and cognition stated, "Marijuana can damage cognitive functioning in adolescents by disrupting the normal development of the white- matter that brains cells need to communicate with each other". This determination concurs with researchers at Northwestern University, Feinberg School of Medicine, which found that there are lasting changes in the "working memory", as it is termed, and critical to memory and reasoning in the adolescent. It must be remembered that all known studies on cognitive function have concluded that the working memory is a strong predictor of academic achievement.

Despite evidence of the negative effects by marijuana use on the adolescent brain, children and adults who have what has been termed intractable epilepsy, which does not respond to standard anti- seizure medications, are treated with a strain of marijuana known as Charlotte's Web to control seizures. This cannabinoids is a purified compound derived from cannabis. Charlotte's Web is available in liquid form in Colorado.

One company called GW Pharmaceuticals is manufacturing a new drug, derived from cannabinoids called Epidiolex. This derivative excludes tetrahydrocannabinol- the compound that makes people feel high. Despite manufacturing this product, Annie Sneed of Scientific American and other researchers admitted and stated that they "do not understand exactly how cannabinoid functions as an anticonvulsant". It works but how it works is yet to be understood.

Common sense would, therefore, dictate and advocate using a beneficial product that alleviates stress, pain, and which provides comfort. This common sense approach has been used, and implicitly condoned by ultra-marathoners, despite USA Track &Field, which governs distance running America, and banning marijuana use by athletes. Canadian snowboarder, Ross Rebagliati, and mixed martial arts fighter Nick Diaz, and NFL wide receiver, Nate Jackson, to name a few, have admitted to using marijuana for the alleviation of pain. Jenn Shelton, an ultra -marathoner, stated, "Pot does all three things (alleviates stress, pain, and nausea)", and Dr. Lynn Webster, founder of the Lifetree Pain Clinic in Salt Lake City, stated, "Cannabinoids block the physical input of pain".

Interesting enough, the World Anti—Doping Agency in 2013 raised the allowable level of THC-the active ingredient- to an amount that would trigger positive results only in athletes consuming marijuana in competition. In a disingenuous manner, the World Anti-Doping Agency has made it acceptable for marijuana to be used by athletes during training, and implicitly places marijuana in the same category as all acceptable painkillers.

Common sense would also dictate strident regulations by the federal government and monitoring by a non-partisan entity and free of lobbyists to bring acceptability to the Herb! However, common sense became trapped and dictated by envy and greed in Colorado, as entrepreneurs with creative ideas, tailored their business plans to capture a niche market in pot-laced drinks, and confections- from chocolates to gummy fish to cheesecakes and edible marijuana. Because of the nascent desire for the legalization of marijuana, there has been no real entity designed to monitor the creative propensity and thirst of the entrepreneur. It was free for all participation and scramble for market share in anticipation of federal approval hence.

It appeared that the rush to capture market share was truncated by greed, limited thought, and scrutiny at every level of responsibility. Local governments in Colorado, in a very simplistic manner, only required sellers of edible marijuana to label the amount of marijuana each serving contained. They even stated that the amount "should not exceed and must be the same potency as a joint". Who is watching the hen house? Colorado restricts the amount of marijuana's main psychoactive ingredient, tetrahydrocannabinol, or THC to 10 milligrams in edibles per serving. Sounds good, but a serving was not specific.

Here is the problem.

A pan of brownies can have five servings of 10 milligrams each of THC, which immediately gives access to consumer 50 milligrams of THC. The distinction should have been made that the total number of units of THC per box is 10 milligrams. Clearly, such an arbitrary approach, not only implied myopic analysis and superficial assessment of a product entering the market place, but a total frenzy where everyone joined the cause of stupidity to endanger life itself.

Colorado has seen the effects of their failure to recognize the propensity of skillful entrepreneurs to satisfy their appetite for profits. Colorado has also seen the effects of their failure to determine what constitutes a serving by teenagers who ate too many crackers and subsequently treated at local hospital emergency rooms. Dan Frosch of the Wall Street Journal reported that the Rocky Mountain Poison and Drug Center, Colorado's poison-control facility, received 79 calls regarding edible marijuana incidents of overdoses in 4 months since legalization.

Compounding the problems associated with marijuana use by adolescents, is the generally accepted practice of combining nicotine products such as, cigarettes or tobacco leaf or sweet tasting and smelling blends of tobacco with the marijuana. It is now a generally accepted practice by the marijuana smoking population that marijuana has to be rolled, not in cigarette rolling paper, such as the popular Big Bambu brand, but in a tobacco leaf or its derivatives. Marijuana is not the only thing that is being smoked, but a combination of nicotine additives.

The smoking of pure marijuana is now seen as "old school", referring to an older generation, but the old school of participants have also joined the millennium and are now combining marijuana with tobacco, or its derivatives, which are composed of nicotine.

I refer to this behavior as the Zeitgeist of a new generation that breeds dependency.

The most commonly used substance to blend the marijuana with, before smoking it, is called fronto. The latter is a leaf of tobacco in its pure form and can be purchased cheaply from any corner store. This product is packaged as innocuous and appealing to the taste buds with an assortment of tastes. The marijuana when rolled with fronto becomes an irregular shaped smoking instrument. It has been reported that this combination increases potency by "adding to the high". The latter is simply the effects of the nicotine product in combination with the marijuana that was smoked. This indulgence is not marijuana in its natural form, but a combination of nicotine and THC. This activity contributes significantly, because of the presence of the highly addictive nicotine, to dependency.

In New York City, where cigarette breaks are allowed but not inside public businesses, smoking has become the outdoor activity According to New York Department of Health and Mental Hygiene and the Centers for Disease Control and Prevention (U.S), in 2013, 16.1% of the city's residents smoke.

Years ago while doing a field visit, I encountered an adolescent who was in the act of massaging marijuana buds that she would place in a piece of tobacco leaf. She was very selective as she carefully examined several pieces of torn leaves. For her, the piece of tobacco leaf she wanted had to be dark brown and translucent; the smell needed a distinct aroma that she had acclimated over time; the amount of moisture content had be exact to encase the marijuana during the rolling process.

Throughout the selection process, she smiled intermittingly, and exhibited her approval of the quality by smelling the pieces in her hand and nodding her head in approval. She did the same with the buds of marijuana that had a distinct aroma- it stunk. I could see from her body and facial expressions complete approval as she placed the piece of torn tobacco leaf into a sheet of rolling paper; a few crushed buds of marijuana was next placed on the tobacco leaf. The mixed preparation became a layer of paper, tobacco, and marijuana. She blended the mixture with the kind of precision used in dentistry and with the final changes of the French painter Paul Gauging.

With precision, her tongue flicked out in a folded form. This female adolescent then inserted the joint quickly between the fold of her tongue and moisturized it with a rotating action. She lit the creation and declared, "dis ah de lick", as her final seal of approval, as she inhaled and filled her lungs with smoke.

A time bomb that brews addiction and dependency was created.

Because of this phenomenon, efforts must be made by clinicians during rehabilitation of addicts and alcoholics, to point out the addictive and damaging effects of nicotine use by their clients. At the same time, the promotion of non-tobacco products with nicotine as the main ingredient must be emphasized by the federal government as simply dangerous and destructive. We cannot continue with the chicken and egg arguments if we are truly committed to stopping the use of cigarettes and its main ingredient nicotine. Some progress has been made but impeded by special interest groups and lobbyists and politicians who are supported by tobacco growers.

Because it was recognized, but not emphasized, that the main culprit that leads up to addiction and dependency remains nicotine, a new twist has developed as an interdiction effort, and as a misnomer called Marijuana Anonymous- 12 Step Program for Marijuana Addicts. This approach, similar to AA and NA, subscribes to the adage that, "no human power can relieve our addiction and that a Higher Power can and will if sought" whereby faith becomes the evidence of things not seen, as stated in Hebrews 11:1. However, relying on intervention by the Higher Power, as the shield to fend off addiction and dependency and to provide the strength needed for daily survival falls short of the commitment and effort needed in addressing the nature of the problem- dependency and a lack of personal responsibility.

I must say that rehabilitation programs do provide good and meaningful guidelines to navigate the pathway towards sobriety and a drug free existence. Programs detail what to expect while detoxifying from marijuana, which has not been determined as addictive, but fail to identify the addictive nicotine. The focus continues to be the process of detoxifying THC from the system that results in insomnia, symptoms of depression, nightmares and vivid dreams, anger, loss of concentration, eating problems, nausea, chronic fatigue, loss of appetite, and withdrawals, but not from nicotine, when nicotine had been demonstrated and known scientifically as addictive. The emphasis must be on nicotine, which has no yielding heath benefit, while marijuana, which has provided a source of healing, looked at in a more positive manner. Programs that do not adequately address the real issues associated with withdrawal from nicotine, as being the real issue for the addicted tobacco user, must shift their thinking.

E-CIGARETTES- INSIDUOUS TECHNOLOGY

Since 1971, the FDA placed a ban on advertising cigarettes. This ban resulted from the known associative dangers from smoking tobacco and a direct contribution to lung cancer. However, there was not a ban on nicotine directly. Nor were there any future interdiction efforts by the federal government or pharmaceutical companies or drugstores to encourage people to stop smoking by not selling cigarettes.

In New York State 52 % of all pharmacies, sell tobacco products-CVS remains the exception. A few other pharmacies are now considering, because of public outcry and contradiction in their approaches to heath, that a new face must be presented to the public and shareholders. However, the profits generated from the sale of cigarettes continue to climb and accounts for 20% of revenue. The issue and quagmire for pharmacies have become one of presenting a face that must depict a semblance of being accountable and in the interest of heath and not their returns on investment. It is a tough call for the small entrepreneur.

Health institutions for patient care are also guilty of practicing unhealthy living, as do pharmacies that sell cigarettes, by preparing unhealthy foods in their cafeterias and for patients under their care. It is not uncommon to see white bread, cereal made with bleached flour, juices of less than 20% composition of real fruit, and excessive salt and sugar content served to patients recuperating in a hospital setting. It does not take a genius to see on public display the trays of fried chicken, poor quality pieces of meats prepared with salt dominant ingredients that contribute to obesity and hypertension. There seems to be an emphasis on taste and not health. It is a difficult call again when profits are paramount for the entrepreneur.

It seems as if the components of the substance negates the dangerous ingredient, and in this case nicotine, from any discussion by making such a distinction, there seems to be a contradiction between cigarettes, which are composed of nicotine and other chemicals, and purified nicotine that is dispensed by another mechanism called the e-cigarette. Then the so-called ban on advertising tobacco products is not on nicotine but on other components of cigarettes.

This approach by the FDA, in my opinion, is a direct endorsement of addiction and an addictive substance by the very agency in charge of a sector of our health. At the same time, the endorsement of nicotine gives authenticity, fuel, and power to advertise an addictive substance. This distorted thinking seems insane and ludicrous.

To add to the insanity, confusion continues and persists despite having concurrent and supportive research on the dangerous effects of nicotine use. To add implicit endorsement and support of nicotine, the FDA (Food and Drug Administration) has failed to regulate e-cigs as a drug-delivery devices because e-cigs has three main ingredients-nicotine, flavoring, and propylene glycol. It seems that the focus is always away from the main ingredient, nicotine, and remains on cigarettes as the issue.

Despite prior court rulings that financially settled cases that resulted from cigarette damages, a federal appeals court ruling in December 2010 stated that the FDA lacked authority over e-cigs. The court expressly stated that the device is not problematic, "because they offer only the recreational benefits of a regular cigarette". Here we go again, and again, by moving the discussion away from the main ingredient and away from research findings on nicotine. The lobbyists are what they do best, and in the interest of their shareholders, and not the health interest of the already addicted. This is simply asinine.

To see the insanity at work, the 2013 Super Bowl and 2014 Golden Globe Awards bring home the point clearly in governmental approval of nicotine through another delivery system. Electronic cigarettes, or e-cigs, dominated the spotlight in advertisement at both events. We now know, from a recent survey that 60% of Americans are now familiar with e-cigs, because of its adverting dominance during both events. This estimate means that half of the country's more than 40 million smokers have tried an e-cigarette at least once. In 2011, of this estimated smoking population, sales on e-cigarette accounted for $113million. To see the shift in nicotine ingestion, three years later, 2014, tells the story. Sales of e-cigarettes grew to an astounding $482million, according to The Wall Street Journal. The entrepreneur follows the dictates of the consumer by shifting their focus to satisfaction of wants.

Most recently, the Food and Drug Administration, on April 24, 2014, in a very disingenuous manner, went after e-cigarette distribution by placing regulations on its sale to anyone under 18 years old and required makers to gain approval for their products. Here transactions cannot be made with minors, but transactions can be made with adults. Approval implies endorsement, promotion, and regulations. The FDA continues to be supportive, yet specifying, "The nicotine in e-cigarettes is Addictive". The FDA gives warning and approval at the same, as is does with cigarettes, while disapproving television advertising the latter and condoning the use of nicotine in e-cigs. It becomes more confusing as the debate continues on what is established fact on the addictive properties of nicotine. Nicotine is addictive!

To further endorse e-cigarettes and by extension nicotine, taxation is far less than on regular cigarettes at the point of purchase and varying by states. In addition, to add insult to injury, the FDA is requiring manufacturers of e-cigarette to provide scientific evidence to substantiate any claims that e-cigarettes are safer than standard cigarettes. The FDA is simply giving more latitude to cigarette manufacturers who are indirectly involved in financing the production of e-cigarettes. Cigarette manufacturers are seeking another niche market for nicotine as cigarette sales have declined in the United States while increasing in developing economies.

Because of less taxation on e-cigarettes and implicit support by the FDA for e-cigs, manufacturers are free to advertise on any medium. Because of the falling sales of cigarettes in the United States, tobacco companies are once again strategizing to reflect the economics of the market place of investments. Reynolds American, Lorillard, and the Altria Group combined are planning to merge while selling brands to satisfy antitrust regulations. These companies are using growth models and projections to tailor investment for a better return, while saturating and penetrating the market.

[30]The Imperial Tobacco Group, an entity from Britain, that has been having difficulty in gaining market share in the United States, "will take advantage of Reynolds and Lorillard's hunger to merge", according to Steven Davidoff Solomon, professor of law at the University of California, Berkeley. Such an approach will lift profits through cost savings while moving into the e-cigarette market that is growing. Lorillard has already acquired Blue Cigs, the largest American seller of e-cigarettes, which has a 40% market share. It is estimated that the e-cigarette market will surpass regular cigarettes by 2047.

Corporations like Altria Group Inc., Reynolds American Inc., to name the leaders, have already penetrated the market for e-cigarettes by capturing about a quarter of all sales at convenience stores, where seven in 10 regular cigarettes are sold, while remaining dominant with seventy percent of the tobacco market share. It has become a beautiful marriage of cigarettes and e-cigarettes of vaporized nicotine.

That's brings me, once again, to the creative nature of the market place of ideas. Because of the vaporized nature of e-cigarettes, startup companies like Avail Vapor LLC have been formed to distribute the e-liquid flavors to 35,000 shops nationally. The market now stands at $2.5 billion while incubating and giving birth to professional lobbyists to build an argument for e-cigarette indulgence. At the same time, magazine advertisements appearing in "GQ, Vanity Fair, and elsewhere" proliferate, according to The Wall Street Journal.

It would appear that because of the new niche market for e-cigarettes, so-called experts who are supported by the cigarette lobby from tobacco states have joined in the chorus to endorse e-cigarettes. Claims are still being made on the so-called "modestly effective" use by e-cigarettes in smoking cessation. According to findings in New Zealand, published in their medical journal called Lancet, of the 657 people who used e-cigarette, a 7.3% abstinence rate was recorded after six months of use. It seems ludicrous to consider this as any success when it has been documented that in the US there are 480,000 deaths annually from nicotine associative use. People at the FDA are either not thinking, or simply stupid, or playing to the tobacco lobbyist in the producing regions of the US where tobacco is still king.

Not only are the so-called compensated experts at work to promote e-cigarette but academics have joined in supporting the use of e-cigarettes. Dr. David Abrams, professor at Johns Hopkins School of Public Health and research director at Legacy, an anti-tobacco group, believes that the device could wean people from traditional cigarettes. This is only his opinion, based on anecdotal evidence, lacks longitudinal studies to support his conclusion, and is contrary to The World Health Organization opinions.

A United Nations agency, in its appeal, has recommended that, governments must restrict e-cigarette advertising and using flavors like fruit and candy that appeal to youth. Dr. Abrams, despite his anti-tobacco stand, has ignored the World Health Organization and the United Nations agency recommendations, by moving the discussion away from the main ingredient – nicotine-to appease those in their struggle with nicotine addiction.

It would also appear, from observation and anecdotal evidence, that nicotine's addiction is relegated to secondary importance, when issues of addiction and substance abuse are being considered in rehabilitation programs. Those working in the helping professions should set examples of themselves as persons whose non-indulgence of nicotine and nicotine laced products set the standard when providing intervention services to those in need of rehabilitation.

If we consider marijuana independent of associative addictive agents (the combination of marijuana with highly addictive nicotine), the focus and on- going discussion can remain on two important aspects of marijuana- national economics and medical.

REASONS TO LEGALIZE

First, a bird's eye glimpse at the economics of legalizing marijuana in the US and the associative price of keeping marijuana illegal by the government at all levels. It must be understood that neither I, nor the government, nor any other entity, or entities have conclusive data to determine how much is truly spent on anti-marijuana enforcement. When looking at anti-marijuana efforts, and in its totality, we must consider the following:

Costs of active law enforcement
Costs of prosecution and possible appeals
Costs for the indigent defendant built into city, state, and federal
    budgets
Costs vis-a- vis lost taxation, if marijuana is illegal
Costs to foster care and social services for children of
    incarcerated offenders
Costs of incarceration of convicted offenders
Costs associated with dislocation of families due to incarceration
    of caregivers

Therefore, using the criterion listed above, to expound the discussions, what follows are extrapolations from public data.

Many leading economists, including Harvard Economics professor, Jeffrey Miron, concluded that marijuana legalization would create approximately $14 billion savings in revenue benefit every year. It was further estimated that the value of the US Marijuana Crop annually is over $35 billion, and "if legalized but

186

taxed and regulated like other goods" would create billions of dollars in revenue, using the multiplying effects of the market place. It would also contribute to employment and by extension further research in marijuana for additional use in pharmaceuticals.

The US Federal Government spends more than $12 billion per year on drug control programs. This amount does not include spending by state or local governments on rehabilitation programs, police, courts, and prisons. Of the $12 billion spent on drug control programs, Michael Hess of BBS News estimated that "marijuana prohibition in the US" costs $7 billion per year, excluding misdemeanor cases. According to University of Washington Economics professor, Dick Startz, the state of Washington alone would save $105 million a year if marijuana were legally regulated. If we extrapolate from these findings, the nation would benefit almost $1 trillion annually.

Because of these financial estimates, the entrepreneurial spirit of the venture capitalists whose focus gins up the creativity of the human psyche comes alive to provide the fuel capital for investment. Remember, creativity gives life to the unfulfilled dreams of the newly successful, while unimpeded market forces which generates economic growth and success for entrepreneurs of every kind establishes the case for the free competitive market place. The US abounds with reams of such stories.

Most recently, an entrepreneur named Justin Hatfield stated that his aim is "to become the Philip Morris of the American marijuana industry". He envisioned the creation of a new market place because "prohibition is about to pop". Mr. Hatfield was talking about the federal legalization of marijuana and being "positioned intelligently" to reap great profits. He clearly spelt out what we all know about the business instinct of the entrepreneur and what it dictates: location, positioning, and timing to be successful.

Mr. Hatfield makes a great case for positioning and by extension timing. He pointed out that during the 1920's and 1930's, when prohibition was present, risk takers like Joseph Kennedy who invested heavily in alcohol, and received what was then called medicinal liquor permits which secured exclusive rights to brands like Dewar's whisky and Gordon gin. This action by Kennedy propelled him further into the millionaire status. Once again, the entrepreneurial spirit leads to success in the free enterprise system.

With foresight and optimism, Mr. Hatfield has recognized the universal appeal of the herb and the international voices for medical legalization, coupled with the favorable swing mood of the nation towards national legalization. As an entrepreneur, he contemplates doing everything possible to satisfy the appetite for the connoisseur of marijuana. Again, the market mechanism driven by national consensus continues to drive the debate for medical use.

Mr. Hatfield plans to have pot-quality evaluations to eventually selling the plant. So far, he has started a website called Weedmaps. com where, according to him, "medical-marijuana users in California could find doctors and dispensaries, rate them, read reviews and message one another". The site made more than $25 million in 2013 and boasts four million visitors each month. It is simple economics at work.

Because of his entrepreneurial drive and desire to capture market share and build product allegiance, he has initiated and invested in start-up ventures through a company called Ghost Group. This company focuses on technology, software, and hardware to market marijuana like regular products that require nutritional food labeling so that users can know the potency and purity of the drug- tetrahydrocannabinol (THC). Creativity at work with the customer in mind at all times.

In his marketing efforts, Mr. Hatfield intends to accommodate and satisfy the purchaser of marijuana by on the spot evaluation of the potency of any purchase. He is developing a gadget for smartphones to test purity of the product at the point of purchase. It is simple marketing for a new population when we look at the changing times with fiscal restraints.

Most people in the business consider him as a late entrant speculator with innovative approaches in the market place of ideas. Others have gone beyond the local marketing concept by moving globally into non - traditional markets. For the past 11 years, Brent Zettl and Prairie Plant Systems Inc. "cornered the market for governmental-approved medical marijuana in Canada", as most people described both companies. Indeed, Canada has seized on the opportunity to market the product to their changing demographics.

It must be pointed out that in Canada, new laws enacted in 2014, are federally regulated and uniform throughout the country. In the United States, we have state rights and federal regulations operating autonomously and adding confusion to the discussion of legal medical marijuana. Canada has even gone further by making it legal for any licensed company to grow and distribute medical marijuana to patients, but illegal for patients to grow their own.

Because of the new laws in Canada, 12 more companies have been granted licenses by Health Canada to grow and distribute medical marijuana. Peace Naturals Project Inc., a medical marijuana company based in Clearview, Ontario, is using Israeli technology to grow and distribute medical marijuana in rural British Columbia. The company also plans to grow its marijuana in a former Hersey's chocolate factory outside Ottawa and, according to reports from Canada directly across the street from a police station. Location, safety, and protection ruled in the selection process.

In Connecticut, growers are cultivating marijuana for medical use in buildings with the exacting standards of pharmaceutical factories. Marijuana production is now cultivated in a controlled setting so that monetary appropriations can be diverted to more meaningful undertakings like education and housing. Currently 47.4 % of drug arrests are for marijuana only, and this accounts for 12.7 % of the inmate population in New York State. Because of the associative costs of incarceration coupled with budgetary and fiscal issues, former New York City Comptroller, John Liu, on August 14, 2013 called for a tax to regulate marijuana sale through decriminalization. John Liu was thinking economics.

Diane Savino of Staten Island sponsored the legalization bill, known as the Compassionate Care Act of 2014 for medical marijuana legality. It should be noted that this bill was previously presented on four different occasions and failed to reach the Senate. Gov.

Andrew Cuomo of New York stated that he is in favor of having a pilot program for medical marijuana distribution to 20 hospitals around the state.

Approval of medical marijuana in New York State is sought from the Food and Drug Administration and this is likely to be granted. Most recently, June 2015, applications to cultivate, manufacture, and dispense medical marijuana were handed out by the State Health Department, and would grant five licenses requiring a bond of $2 million. The law calls for the drug to be available in January 2016. Most of the farming would be in places like Wallkill, Orange County.

Interestingly enough, once the FDA grants its imprimatur signature, Washington becomes impotent to withdraw medical grants extended to the state, despite marijuana being illegal under federal law. This is a very creative and ingenuous way to move forward with access to medical marijuana. In addition to seeking FDA approval for medical marijuana, the governor became more creative in his support by signing into state law The Compassionate Care Act on July 5, 2014 with the following stipulations:

1. Marijuana banned from smoking in all public places.
2. Individual dosing of medical cannabis to be mandated and its purity in all forms, such as capsules, made known.
3. Precise amounts based on patient's response.
4. Metered dosing that gives flexibility to add cannabis to other therapies.
5. Marijuana treated like all medicines.

The governor is making the connection to economics and the market place of creative ideas as Mr. Hatfield, who has focused his entrepreneurial skills into dosing and purity issues to guarantee that it is free of contaminants. Individual doses and packages would be medically graded and affixed with bar codes that make packaging easily tracked.

Here we see that the governor is supportive of moving the product to a medical supply-chain that considers public safety, regulatory and law-enforcement inputs. The governor is also responding to the Drug Enforcement Administration position, which states, "Medical marijuana programs do not meet standards of modern medicine because they lack standardized composition or dosage." The FDA is still moving around in circles with regressive thinking.

While New York City continues the debate on the definition of marijuana possession as a crime, if indeed there is, on a local level, the election of Mayor de Blasio in 2014, has given hope for true change. He campaigned and pledged to repair relations between police and minority residence, who are the most affected, with the debate focused on possession of marijuana. The debate continues in state after state.

It has been proposed that those found in possession of small amounts of marijuana would not be subjected to an arrest but would be issued a ticket, similar to one that is issued for a parking violation. Ticket issued to those found in possession of small amounts of marijuana- 25 grams or less- has led the debate that considers the character and integrity of the individual who uses the substance. Yet this approach, disappointedly upholds the punitive federal role while disassociating administrative costs associated with low level crime pegged to people with no prior criminal record. It has become the analysis without thought, and as the philosopher Nietzsche stated, "there are no facts, only interpretations." All states continue to interpret the federal law and with more insight in a pragmatic manner.

This has been the first time that any consideration has been given to the damaging social effect, when conviction for this federally defined illicit substance, becomes public record and accessible to all. Just using officers to arrest and transport a person found in possession of small amounts of marijuana, and then fingerprinting that person, sets in motion a criminal record with lasting ramifications that jeopardizes personal advancement.

The new proposal that takes into account the possession of small quantities warranting the issuance of a violation ticket compounds the issue if that person is smoking the substance in public and the quantity remains within the permissible range of 25 grams and under. The new proposal suggests that smoking the substance in public constitutes a violation, while knowing that possession by extension infers smoking or usage of the substance does not qualify for an arrest.

On the other hand, the new proposal allows for an arrest if the person was observed smoking in public or is found in possession, but cannot produce an acceptable identification. Although the proposal allows for another person to produce acceptable identification, at the local precinct, for those arrested for possession, it remains firm on creating a criminal charge for smoking in public. Neither proposal seems acceptable, especially for those without any prior criminal record or a young adult. Let the relationship between the public and citizens remain an honest one where dialogue can ameliorate the interactions between both parties.

Rather, as proposed, a ticket of $100 should be issued for the first time offense and a second offense in three years $250. According to the NYPD, the issuing of a summons would no longer track the race and ethnicity of the recipient. However, the recording of the issuance of a summons for a violation would still influence the behaviors of authorities towards the punitive position. I propose, no recording of a judicial decision, while treating the violation just like an opened can of beer.

In Colorado, the state's higher court is poised to decide whether employers are required or allowed to permit citizens to use marijuana while in their employment. A law suit was brought by a medicinal marijuana user who was fired for failing an employment drug test in 2010, despite Colorado permitting medical marijuana in 2000, and legalized marijuana for recreational use in 2012, but prohibited under federal law. Just the thought of trying to understand the nuances of the law makes little sense.

We also know that in California there are currently 45,000 drug offenders in prison for extended periods, and that 80 % are low-level offenders with convictions for possession and sale of small amounts of marijuana. The cost to California is approximately $1 billion annually ($80,000 annually per prisoner) including tracking persons on parole for marijuana conviction, urine testing, and administrative costs.

In March 2014, former Attorney General Eric Holder called for reduction of sentences for defendants in most of the nation's drug cases in conjunction with reserving stiff penalties for most violent traffickers of illicit drugs, as part of his effort to cut U.S prison population. This approach would affect 70 % of drug offenders in the criminal justice system and by extension reduce spending on petty crime prevention associated with marijuana conviction. Let us hope his successor, Loretta Lynch, is instrumental in the continued fight for federal legalization.

Prior to this approach, he announced during August of 2013 the following: low-level non-violent drug offenders with no connection to gangs or large scale drug organizations would not be automatically charged with offenses that call for severe mandatory sentences. Unlike the irreparable damage, that the Rockefeller Law did in New York State this approach would affect more than 216,000 federal inmates, half of whom are serving time for drug-related crimes. An approach whose time has finally come after incubating too long while young futures remain in limbo, as they age beyond their productive years.

Dr. Eric Charles from American University presented two important questions, not answered about incarceration of non –violent offenders convicted for marijuana possession and sale. The questions are as follows:

1. How does it help society to put those people behind bars?
2. Whom are we protecting by segregating people who do not pose a danger to the people or property around them?

Dr. Charles answered the questions by stating "society benefits when people who deserve to be sent to prison are sent to prison, the private prison system benefits when anyone is sent to prison". An interesting observation at our slow progress keeping pace with other countries that is quickly moving in the direction of containment of a range of illicit drugs instead of incarceration.

MEDICINAL MARIJUANA

Medical marijuana remains as controversial as the chicken and egg discussion. Let us look at some opinions.

In 2006, the US Food & Drug Administration issued an advisory on cannabis, which stated, "marijuana has a high potential for abuse; has no currently accepted medical use in treatment in the United States, and has a lack of acceptable safety for use under medical supervision".

This edict was followed with an announcement by the National Institute on Drug Abuse which stated that "marijuana itself" is an unlikely medication candidate for the following reasons:

(a) It is an unpurified plant containing numerous chemicals with unknown health effects.
(b) It is typically consumed by smoking and further contributing to potential adverse effects.
(c) Its cognitive impairing effects may limit its utility.

In 2007, the American Glaucoma Society stated that marijuana "showed potential therapeutic value in that it helps lower intraocular pressure" in the eye. However, the society recommended against its use because of "its side effects and short duration of action and the lack of evidence that its use alters the course of glaucoma". However, anecdotal evidence of lowering ocular pressure and its relationship to glaucoma was never given any credence.

Talking about anecdotal evidence, this brings me to a close associate with whom many exhaustive hours were spent, before his demise, debating numerous issues and in particular those in the medical community. He was diagnosed with glaucoma more than twenty years ago by a young foreign medical student from the Middle East.

During his short life, he subscribed to the healing properties of the body and made the connection between the elements within the universe to create the balance required for existence. He subscribed to the dietary laws as enumerated in the old testament of the Holy Bible, to the eradication of Buddha's three Poisons of Man: Greed, Anger, and Ignorance. He practiced good and never envied and was responsible for all his actions. He found himself in an avalanche of self-centered folks in today's impulsive society. Poorly functioning eyes were an interruption in his life.

He kept all his optical appointments with precision. His eyes were very important. He depended on them and was lost on a psychological level without good functioning eyes. Eyes gave vision and, at times confirmed suspicion, by providing evidence that the mind conjures. Eye problems began in his adolescent years that subsequently led to prescription eye glasses. Coke bottle lenses. Yes, myopia, and more who knows what. His eye doctors were never accurate. He knew they were guessing. Nevertheless, they wrote very puzzling prescriptions that only provided shortly good vision that satisfied him to do the things that brought happiness.

I was told that he had numerous and varying prescriptions written by known, recognized, and eminent ophthalmologists, and a few professors at teaching medical institutions. On one occasion, a professor of optics admitted to her paucity of knowledge, not experience, in treating persons like him with ongoing and changing vision every few months- every contact with whoever was his new ophthalmologist resulted in a new prescription. He dutifully filled every prescription. But every newly filled prescription lasted a few weeks and he was back to what he called "square one". The process continued for years as he became frustrated with all clinicians whom he knew were baffled with his eye condition. Luckily, his introduction to marijuana by a local Rastafarian, while skeptical of its healing properties, proved to be the elixir needed.

I recall vividly what he was told by the local Rastafarian about his relationship and balance of the universe with contributing natural herbs. I found it interesting that the Rastafarian differentiated himself from the dreadlocks, those with hair grown as symbols of style not thought, whom he ascribed to being in disunity with the laws of nature and the universe. For him, the properties of nature found in the marijuana, not a combination of THC with nicotine is the basis of the balancing properties, and hence controlling ocular pressure. He issued a stern warning of the "evil in the bottle", as he referred to alcohol, and the problems of western medicine dissociating healing from the natural process, which was granted to humans by The Unifying force.

Since his introduction to marijuana and until his demise, he continued using the substance, attending all required eye appointments for the measuring of optical pressure. His physician complimented his adherence to the prescribed drug. Indeed, he was using marijuana more frequently than he was using the prescribed drug- a bottle of 20 drops lasted 20 days, if used as prescribed- but he was using 20 drops every two months.

EVIDENCE ENOUGH PRESENTED?

In March, 2011The American Society of Addiction Medicine issued a white paper recommending a halt to the use of marijuana as medication in the US, even in states where it has been declared legal. The Institute of Medicine and the U.S. Food and Drug Administration, and the National Institute on Drug Abuse, concurred in their opinions, that there is no medicinal value for marijuana use. Nevertheless, they all agree and qualified their opinions and recommended its use where "nausea, appetite loss, pain, and anxiety can be mitigated by cannabis" and where "there was no alternative".

On the one hand, there is total condemnation of marijuana in all its phases, while on the other hand there is support for marijuana's use for numerous conditions. Oddly enough, medical cannabis has been described by many physicians during their practice as, "somewhat effective in chemotherapy induced nausea and vomiting and may be a reasonable option for those who do not improve following preferential treatment". They are all agreeing that there is usage for medical marijuana, as seen and experienced in their medical practice.

To add more confusion to the discussion on medical application of marijuana, The American Medical Association, Leukemia & Lymphoma Society, and American Academy of Family Physicians, concurs in their approval of marijuana use under medical supervision. Yes, medical supervision, and more support. Most recently, during March 2014, the federal government signed off on a study that uses marijuana to treat veterans with PTSD. To support this action, the Department of Health &Human Services went beyond the federal action and cleared the way for the purchase of medical marijuana. Yes, there is usage for medical marijuana.

Now the same federal government that assigned marijuana to a Schedule 1 substance under federal Government Controlled Substance Act, which categorized marijuana as having a high-risk for abuse with no acceptable medical application, is repealing itself by allowing its use for seizures and PTSD. These agencies, once again, continue to exemplify the retrograde thinking that flourishes in the chain link of bureaucratic controls where lines of power and control remain in academic discussions. The bureaucrats will beat an issue or a subject to death with debates, discussions, expert input, and pending conclusion to an obvious solution.

Some progress.

Progress, only in the sense that this easing up and keeping at bay the application of punitive actions, allows persons like University of Arizona Professor Suzanne Sisley to measure the effects of five different potencies of smoked or vaporized marijuana in treating PTSD in 50 veterans. The Veterans Administration estimated that 10-20% of veterans- 7.7 million- have PTSD. What thinking takes place when the remedy to alleviate pain is available but not conclusively approved by consensus? It becomes a difficult decision when scientific training truncates evidence.

In the international arena, medical use of cannabis has been legalized in Austria, Belgium, Canada, Finland, Israel, Netherland, Spain, Uruguay, and the United Kingdom. Although cannabis is legal in some states in the US, it remains illegal under US federal law. The United Kingdom has gone even further in their thrust to find new medicines for numerous ailments by designing plants, through hybrid manipulations, and in this case marijuana, to treat crones disease, glaucoma, epilepsy and other diseases that are not responsive to current treatments. The United Kingdom has contracted G.W Pharmaceuticals to grow and design specific strains of marijuana for medical use.

While these countries have made marijuana legal, not only for medical conditions, but for general consumption, the National Institutes of Health holds a US patent for medical cannabis. The patent is entitled: Cannabinoids as antioxidants and neuro-protectants. The patent was issued in October 2003. Economics at work by the National Institutes of Health with a focus of control at all levels of the marijuana sectors in the United States. It then seems logical, given governmental deficits (state, local, and federal) and the probability of raising the debt ceilings that would further exacerbate indebtedness to future generations, a case can be made for the legalization and usage of marijuana in the United States by segments of the population just as is cigarettes is available throughout the nation and universally.

For the experts in their respective fields to keep their heads buried in the sand of paralysis of the analysis, yet governed by the funding of intricate hedge funds and private-equity firms, I contend, is to exhibit a paucity of understanding of the importance that finances play in the economy.

Secondly, since there is anecdotal and contradictory evidence coming from medical communities in the U.S and foreign countries attesting to the benefits of marijuana for numerous illnesses, access must be made simple for persons in need, when there is no other alternative, as suggested by experts. It is humane and it is economics.

Not only were names being created and assigned to specific strains of marijuana, but also the competitive spirit of capitalism remained at work bringing out the genius of the individual producer. Names such as, Purple Drink, Pineapple Express, and Rags, just to name a few, have become common for the acclimated taste buds of active participants who are selective. It has been reported that specific strains of marijuana have been grown for Guns& Roses-rock band- by a partnership called Kushman Veganics. We now have Cannabis Cup competition is Seattle, Washington State, under the name Veganic Chernobyl (GT).

The economics of marijuana, as it continues the journey for approval, implicitly through taxation, has now arrived on Oregon's Measure 91, which proposed a state tax on marijuana producers that would be lower than in states such as Colorado and Washington and where taxes in both states are still comparatively high at 44% and 30% respectively. This approach, according to state officials, is being considered to stymie the incentive for black market sales of marijuana, where taxes are non- existent. Then the question becomes, why tax growers at the production level instead of at the corporate level earnings and at the consumption level where the consumer determines demand? Dae Kopilak, a corporate lawyer, answers the question by stating that the setting of the tax rate is a "balancing act between maximizing revenue, discouraging underage use and eliminating the black market".

According to the Rand Drug Policy Research Center, early projections of revenues, through taxation, have failed to materialize in both states where marijuana is legal. This is so because bureaucrats and policy makers are yet to understand the correlation between high taxes at the producers' level and high prices at legal pot shops and making the black market a cheaper alternative, as suggested by some. However, the black market for marijuana can succumb to an early death by having a negligible consumption tax that does not grant an incentive to make a purchase from an illegal source.

ALERT

Former President, Richard Nixon, fed up with all the discussions and efforts at eradicating drugs from the lives of Americans, declared The War on Drugs, in his speech to the Nation, on June 17, 1971, when he stated: "America's public enemy number one in the United States is drug abuse. In order to fight and defeat this enemy, it is necessary to wage a new, all-out offensive". As he declared war, the innovative producers became more creative with new methods and approaches to satisfying the needs of addicts while remaining ahead of the law.

From the market place of creative ideas and innovation that brought financial rewards for ingenuously remaining on the offensive, to creating new formulas with thousands of variations for drugs, yet to be declared illegal, became the indulgences of chemists around the world. It became the cat and mouse game as chemists got busy changing the chemical formulae of drugs, which were declared illegal, to unknown entities to evade authorities and to satisfy the demands for illicit drugs. Out of the chemical laboratories, synthetic marijuana emerged for global consumption targeting the unsuspecting and uninformed user who placed satisfaction before heath.

Synthetic Cannabis aka Synthetic Marijuana, disingenuously called marijuana replacements, which were legal, and having since been banned in numerous localities, arrived on the scene with attractive sounding names like K2, Spice, Yucatan Fire, Skunk, Herbal Smoking Blends, Genie, Moon Rocks, and Black Mamba. Spice, was later found to be dangerous and powerful, smoked very much like marijuana. Aided by the internet, Spice, like other named substitutes, became reachable to everyone on the planet who had access to a computer.

The designing of specialty drugs was the handiwork of John William Huffman, Professor Emeritus in organic chemistry at Clemson University in South Carolina. He and his colleagues, created over 400 synthetic cannabinoid compounds. Synthetic Cannabis arrived in the early 2000's. It was promoted as having the same effects as naturally grown marijuana, because it was believed to be a mixture of natural herbs. However, laboratory analysis in 2008 determined that the mixture called and sold as Synthetic Marijuana was a designer drug in which herbs, incense, and leafy materials were sprayed with liquid chemicals to mimic the effect of tetrahydrocannabinol (THC), the psychoactive ingredient in naturally grown marijuana plant(cannabis sativa)". This mixture was legally sold in convenience stores, smoke shops, and on line until July 2012. Nevertheless, this lethal mixture is still available on line in various municipalities because of current and indecisive laws.

However, the popular belief persists that synthetic marijuana is safe, non-toxic, and according to observers, "elicits psychoactive (mind-altering) effect similar to regular marijuana". This word of mouth acceptance has kept the mixture easily available to teenagers. It has been reported by Monitoring the Future 2011 that 11% of teenager reported using synthetic marijuana, while 36% of high school seniors reported using natural marijuana.

This toxic mixture has resulted in numerous emergency room treatments throughout the country. The 2012 DAWN Report from the U.S Substance Abuse and Mental Health Services Administration (SAMHSA) stated that toxicity due to synthetic marijuana resulted in 11,400 cases of emergency visits in 2010. Users have reported psychotic effects like extreme anxiety, paranoia, and hallucinations, nausea, vomiting, agitation and seizures.

Mike Powers, author of Drugs Unlimited, reported that chemists are now sending their receipts off to Chinese chemical factories to make new compounds to avoid detection when exported to foreign countries, including the United States. Mike Powers stated that in 2010 there were 49 brand new legal psychoactive drugs invented, while in 2012 there were 57 newer drugs formulated and advertised on the Internet. This creation is the direct result of the innovative spirit of the entrepreneur that is driven by demand. The internet social media marketing effort clearly demonstrates the universal vulnerability all nations are faced with in all sectors of every society.

SUMMATION

The currently designed approaches leading to sobriety for alcoholics and a substance free existence for drug addicts are all stuck in a paralysis of the analysis of study after study. As studies progress, those in the helping professions continue to witness marginal and minimal success with their approaches at rehabilitating both populations. Yet, the focus and thrust of treatment remain ingrained with the psychological problems of the abusers. Little attention is paid to the permanent physiological changes in the body and its effect on dependency and addiction. It is time to think out of the box.

It is time for a new consideration, and acceptance of the word functional with the appendage of alcoholic or addict. The acceptance must be made without a meaning that adds carnage to the perception of the individual, and whose system has been transformed by metabolic adaptation in the liver and molecular changes in the brain, for their difficulties in breaking drug and alcohol habits. Moreover, if we can inculcate functional with cognition that places less emphasis on mental problems, but dependent on needs by using alternative approaches, then there is hope.

Not only is there a need for emphasis on the physiological, but also an understanding of the role of CRF (Corticotrophin Response Factor), and the direct contribution it plays in addiction and dependency. Let us continue exploring this link as the alternative approach in addressing alcoholism, and with a goal of developing medications for the treatment of addictive disorders. We must also recognize that, although the psychological plays only a minimal but important role in the struggle of the alcoholic, it must be addressed in the here and now.

Cocaine and heroin remain in the battleground for ingrained addiction and dependency. Cocaine remains a problem and presents challenges for the addict and pharmaceuticals researchers as the battle continues. Dr. Barbara Mason, co-director of the Pearson Center for Alcoholism and Research at the Scripps Research Institute in La Jolla, California stated that because "there is no known effective prescription medicine for treating cocaine addiction" more research appropriations should be available for pharmaceutical intervention, not as a cure, but as the buoy, that establishes functionality.

Heroin is now raising its ugly head again, and adhering to the market forces of price and substitution effect. It is the substitute for pain addictive medications, once prescribed, that have become prohibitively expensive for the newly minted addicts. More troubling, and for those who became addicted involuntarily and legally through professional interventions, is that they had no choice. Let legal actions proceed against the purveyors of legal addiction.

Chemical-replacement therapies as methadone has become a two edged sword for the addict. Although methadone was described as, "effective at reducing pleasure and blocking cravings for certain opiates", it remains a chemical of dependency for the addict to exist and remain somewhat functional. Most methadone users have indicated that it takes months to become tolerant of methadone while the physical and psychologically yearnings for heroin continue. Methadone is promoted as taking away withdrawals symptoms from opiate addiction, and leading to detoxification. I am yet to see a heroin user who participated in methadone therapy become completely free of opiates.

Many opiate programs are referred to as methadone maintenance. That is all it does, and nothing more than blocking the cravings for most addicts while others continue to dabble intermittently. Methadone has becomes the vehicle which allows opiate abusers to function so that they can provide for themselves the minimum degree of care. Yes, they do function, and in most cases, like zombies. Let research continue for alternatives.

I predict that biotech startups like Cara Therapeutics and pharmaceutical giants like Pfizer Inc., currently working on developing a strong painkiller that does not make people high, will become a reality in less than a decade. Professor Stephen Waxman, a professor of neurology at Yale University School of Medicine stated that such a development would be "a Holy Grail of pain research". This advancement, hopefully, would stymie the ongoing abuses of drugs like morphine, oxycodone, and hydrocodone. Pain would be treated as pain without exposing patients to the euphoric effects of the aforementioned drugs.

Lastly, the economics of marijuana, encompassing financial and medical aspects, must be looked at as seriously as other developed nations are currently doing. Most nations that have legalized marijuana and have integrated and revised their judicial system to address usage, not as violations of the law, but as a vehicle of earnings, can use those earnings to educate and finance long term research on the positive aspects of marijuana. International trade regulations that monitors and controls distribution of marijuana should become standard.

We have to become more progressive towards the acceptance and reality that marijuana is here to stay and will be consumed, as it has been for the past thousand years. We must also bear in mind that there is a plethora of confusing and contradictory information, coming especially from the medical communities and independent experts. Yet, there is concurring agreement that marijuana should be recommended as a therapeutic modality, when there is no other option and this implies a benefit for the user.

Concurring in opinions for the recommending of marijuana for medical reasons suggest that there is limited, yet to be understood, knowledge of marijuana beyond what is now known about the effects on the undeveloped adolescent brain. There seems to be no differentiation of marijuana mixed with tobacco products and the linkage to addiction coming directly from nicotine. There is a need for longitudinal studies on adults smoking only marijuana and a relationship to health.

Anecdotal evidence affirming that marijuana is helpful must be given validity. Unimpeded access to outlets, for those seeking relief from pains and elevated ocular pressure, must be a reality. And, if we are to remain a humane nation that subscribes to freedom of choice without infringing on the rights of others, then the discussion can continue.

We are now beginning to witness the changes that have occurred in the public attitudes to the acceptance of marijuana for medical and recreational uses. We are also seeing state initiatives to decriminalize and subsequently legalize marijuana. However, the federal government remains steadfastly opposed to legalization, while budgeting billions of dollars to keep marijuana illegal by incarcerating non- violent offenders for possession. We can better spend the billions appropriated to keeping marijuana illegal, by placing such funds in education, housing, medical care, and research. New York City has begun the move in this direction to keep the character intact for the user who does not have any criminal backgrounds.

Patrick Kennedy, chairman at Smart Approach to Marijuana, called the ongoing approach to medical marijuana a "public heath debacle" that needs objectivity and reality based reasoning.

We can and must join the developed nations and emerging markets that are restructuring producing methods and implementing quality control to address the international demand of this cash crop. Since this is free enterprise at its best, let economics prevail.

Marijuana is now legal for recreational use in Alaska, Washington State, Oregon, the District of Columbia, the State of Colorado, and legal for medicinal use in New York State. In the not too distant future, all forms of marijuana will be legalized, controlled, and monitored by each state. Medicinal marijuana will no longer be discussed as an academic exercise, but will be viewed as the helping instrument for those whom there is no alternative therapy, as in Israel.

Marijuana will legal under federal law. Accessibility will be for all who choose to indulge without fear of tarnishing their character; minors will not have legal access to the substance. The policy of prohibition against recreational use of marijuana will be overwhelmed by the powerful forces of the market place. The fear of the unknown will disappear and true progress will be made from dialogue and respect for cognitive and rational reasoning. The demonizing, demagoguery, and out of context quoting by professionals to justify their positions will end in collective dialogue on issues of human concerns.

BIBLIOGRAPHY

Extrapolations and quotations herein, are from sources mentioned below. Some references are from historical sources. Most articles were authored for centers for drug addiction and alcohol dependency, and contributions were made to national and international periodicals by the following:

1   Black, M.D., Donald W and Grant, M.D., M.P.H., Jon E. Diagnostic and Statistical Manual of Mental Disorders (DSM-5). Arlington : American Psychiatric Association, 2014. American Psychiatric Association. 1000 Wilson Boulevard, Suite 1825, Arlington, Va. 22209-3901 ph: 703-907-7300 email: apa@psych.org.

2   NYC Administration for Children's Services. [Online] Cited as reference information only. http://www.nyc.gov/html/acs/html/home/home.shtml.

3   NYC Human Resources Administration. [Online] Cited as reference information only. http://www.nyc.gov/html/hra/html/home/home.shtml.

4   Alcoholics Anonymous. [Online] Cited as reference information only. http://www.aa.org/.

5   Narcotics Anonymous. [Online] Cited as reference information only. https://www.na.org/.

6   Mathis, Judge Greg E. Ask Judge Mathis. [Online] Cited as reference information only. http://askjudgemathis.com/.

7   Michigan's 36th District Court. [Online] Cited as reference information only. http://www.36thdistrictcourt.org/.

8   Guildford Castle : Guildford Borough Council. [Online] Cited as reference information only. http://www.guildford.gov.uk/castle.

9   U.S. Securities and Exchange Commission. [Online] Cited as reference information only. http://www.sec.gov/.

10 MFF. [Online] Cited as reference information only. http://www.mff.org/.

11 Zbigniew Brzezinski. Simon & Schuster. [Online] Cited as reference information only. http://authors.simonandschuster.com/Zbigniew-Brzezinski/699164.

12 Peter F. Drucker. HarperCollins US. [Online] Cited as reference information only. http://www.harpercollins.com/cr-102095/peter-f-drucker.

13 Robert A Nisbet. The Sociological Tradition. s.l. : Transaction Publishers, 1993, pp. xxi - xxiii.

14 What the Numbers Show About N.F.L. Player Arrests. Irwin, Neil. s.l. : New York Times Company, 9 12, 2014, New York Times.

15 Gabapentin Treatment for Alcohol Dependence. Barbara J. Mason, PhD (1), et al. 1, s.l. : Author Affiliations - 1: The Scripps Research Institute, Pearson Center for Alcoholism and Addiction Research, La Jolla, California 2: Scripps Clinic and Scripps Green Hospital, La Jolla, California, Jan 2014, JAMA Internal Medicine, Vol. 174, pp. 70-77.

16 Applied Economics. Thomas Sowell | Home. [Online] Cited as reference information only. http://www.tsowell.com/Appliedecon.htm.

17 Alexis de Tocqueville - Wikipedia, the free encyclopedia. Wikipedia. [Online] Ciited as reference information only. http://en.wikipedia.org/wiki/Alexis_de_Tocqueville.

18 Perls, Frederick S. Gestalt Therapy Verbatim. s.l. : Real People Press, 1969. p. 7. ISBN 0-911226-02-8.

19 Sax, Leonard. Wall Street Journal - Leonard Sax. Leonard Sax MD PhD | Physician, Psychologist, and Author. [Online] Quoted from second(2nd) paragraph. http://www.leonardsax.com/wsj.htm.

20 DSM-5: A Manual Run Amok. McHugh, Paul. s.l. : The Wall Street Journal, 5 17, 2013, The Wall Street Journal.

21 American Psychiatric Association: Black, M.D., Donald W; Grant, M.D., M.P.H., Jon E. American Psychiatric Association: Diagnostic and Statistical Manual of Mental Disorders, Fifth Edition. Fift. Arlington : American Psychiatric Publishing, 2013. pp. 66, 122, 708. American Psychiatric Association. 1000 Wilson Boulevard, Suite 1825, Arlington, Va. 22209-3901 ph: 703-907-7300 email: apa@psych.org.

22 A.D.H.D. Seen in 11% of U.S. Children as Diagnoses Rise. Schwarz, Alan and Cohen, Sarah. s.l. : The New York Times Company, April 1, 2013, New York Times, p. A1.

23 How Attention-Deficit Disorder Went Global. Hinshaw, Stephen P and Scheffler, Richard M. s.l. : Dow Jones & Company, Inc, March 11, 2014, The Wall Street Journal.

24 Frances: New psych manual will hike health costs. Frances, Dr. Allen. s.l. : Newsday, January 1, 2013.

25 Substance Abuse and Mental Health Services Administration. Results from the 2011 National. Substance Abuse and Mental Health Services Administration. s.l. : Substance Abuse and Mental Health Services Administration, 2012. NSDUH Series H-44, HHS Publication No. (SMA) 12-4713. - This document is in the Public Domain. (See pg 2 of original doc for public domain release).

26 Rockoff, Jonathan. A Pill to Cure Addiction. *The Wall Street Journal.* December 23, 2013. http://www.wsj.com/articles/SB1000142405270 2304475004579276233917668764.

27 Milam, James R and Ketcham, Katherine. *Under the Influence: A Guide to the Myths and Realities of Alcoholism.* s.l. : Random House Publishing Group, 2011. p. 34. 030780173X, 9780307801739.

28 Tyson, Mike and Sloman, Larry. *Undisputed Truth.* s.l. : Penguin Publishing Group, 2013. ISBN 9780399161285.

29 *MFF - The Milken Family Foundation.* [Online] Cited as reference information only. http://www.mff.org/.

30 Thomas, Katie. Doubts Raised About Off-Label Use of a Painkiller. *The New York Times.* May 14, 2014, p. B1. http://www.nytimes.com/2014/05/14/business/doubts-raised-about-off-label-use-of-subsys-a-strong-painkiller.html?_r=0.

31 Campo-Flores, Arian and Elinson, Zusha. Heroin Use, and Deaths, Rise. *The Wall Street Journal.* Feb 3, 2014. http://www.wsj.com/articles/SB1 0001424052702304851104579361250012275942.

32 Gay, Mara. New York City's Adult Smoking Rate Climbs. *The Wall Street Journal.* Sept 15, 2014. http://www.wsj.com/articles/new-york-citys-adult-smoking-rate-climbs-1410812653.

33 Solomon, Steven Davidoff. With Merger, Tobacco Takes On Technology. *The New York Times.* Jul 12, 2014, p. B2.

ABOUT THE AUTHOR

Wentworth Lionel Carrega is a former senior analyst for AT&T. He worked in the Department of Social Services and the Administration for Children's Services for two decades. The author is the recipient of the United States of America Congressional Certificate for Children & Education. Amazon.com cited the author as providing The Most Helpful Critical Review for Soros Lectures. He received five star ratings for his reviews of Malcolm X and Duty. He earned his BSC and MBA degrees from Fordham University and studied urban education at the Graduate School of Education, Brooklyn College, and counseling at the Graduate School of Guidance & Counseling of the City of New York, Hunter College.

www.ingramcontent.com/pod-product-compliance
Lightning Source LLC
Chambersburg PA
CBHW031506270326
41930CB00006B/271